Midnight Mass:

Poetic Scripture for the Broken Soul

Author: Daniel Villanueva
Illustrated by: Sarah Fazriah

Table of Contents

Foreword... 5

Chapter 1: Genesis

The Fifth Element 15

The Artist 19

Desire 21

Chapter 2: Descent

The Taste of Death
....27

The Jesters Tango……….....................................31

Possession...33

Pain 35

Rage .... .37

Gritted teeth .... .39

Respite 41

Exorcism... .45

Translation for "Exorcism" (Latin)... 46

Chapter 3: Abyss

Two-Face 51

A Dark Place 55

Essence of Humanity.. 57

Death 63

Hypnosis 67

Skin Walker 71

A Penance Unpaid 75

Spelunking
.... 79

Perseverance 83

Resurrected 85

Chapter 4: Revelation

Revelation 91

Ritual: Heilung
....95

The Shadow 97

The Me 101

Heilung 105

Proto-Germanic Translations for "Ritual: Hei-
lung".. 106

Chapter 5: Ascension

The Horsem.. 111

Hope 115

Illusion 117

Grounded 121

Bones 123

Extra Content...127

Foreword

This poetic collection is something I've wanted to create my entire life. First and foremost, thank you to my mother and father – I would not be here without you. To my siblings: you've been the best friends I could have asked for. Thank you for reading my early poems when I was 15 on those summer nights and letting me explore my voice during that first heartbreak (lol).

Thank you, Ellie, for being open to my work and allowing me the freedom to write without judgment. Your support means the world.
To everyone I've shared my poetry with prior to this point – Thank you for your feedback, critiques, and your kindness.

Thank you to Christy Perez for the chapel photo!
And a very big thank you to Sarah! Creating all the art for this book from every poem to the portrait of me on the back of this book, I'm sure it was no easy task and you did phenomenal. I hope you enjoyed reading all the poetry as I enjoyed seeing you develop the art.

You can follow Sarah and her art on Instagram
@voidofdoom__
And
@mvddrak_atmospheric (This style is used through my book)

You can follow Christy and her photography page on Instagram
@lil_hobbit

You can follow my poetry online on Instagram
@Hauntedquills

So, what is this book? Midnight Mass will hopefully push you to face the darkest parts of yourself and face the ugliness we all hold inside while also taking you on a journey through love, loss, despair, hope, and realization. Come face to face with the parts of ourselves that we try to forget or ignore.
We all have to remember that without those parts of us, we would not be who we are today and in accepting those parts of us and healing those traumas, we can become the best version of ourselves possible.

So, without further ado…

Here is Midnight Mass: Poetic Scripture for the Broken Soul.

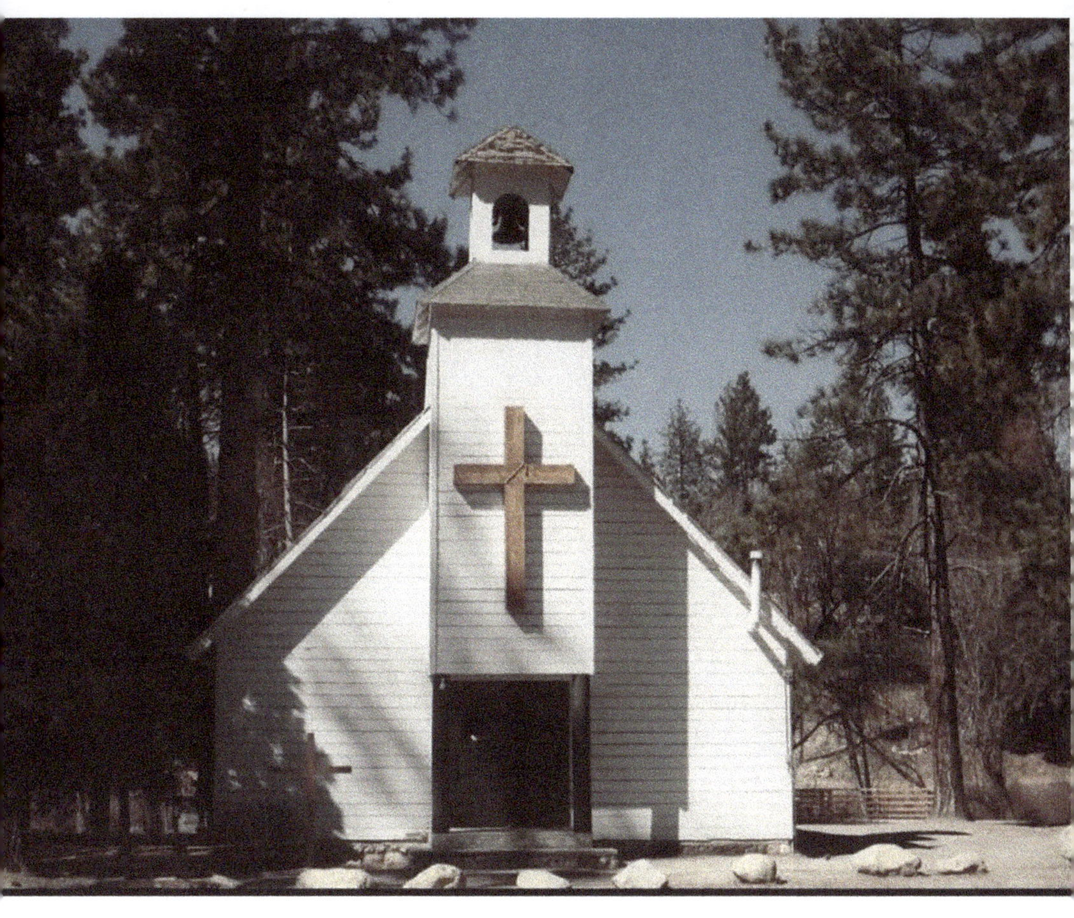

Welcome and enter through these chapel doors,
Do not be afraid.
Something Dark and Vampiric waits for you,
Waiting to escape-
Down in the Abyss of each of our Souls.

Chapter 1: Genesis

In the beginning…
There was love and hope.
Desire and passion burning bright,
Nothing could snuff out the building light…

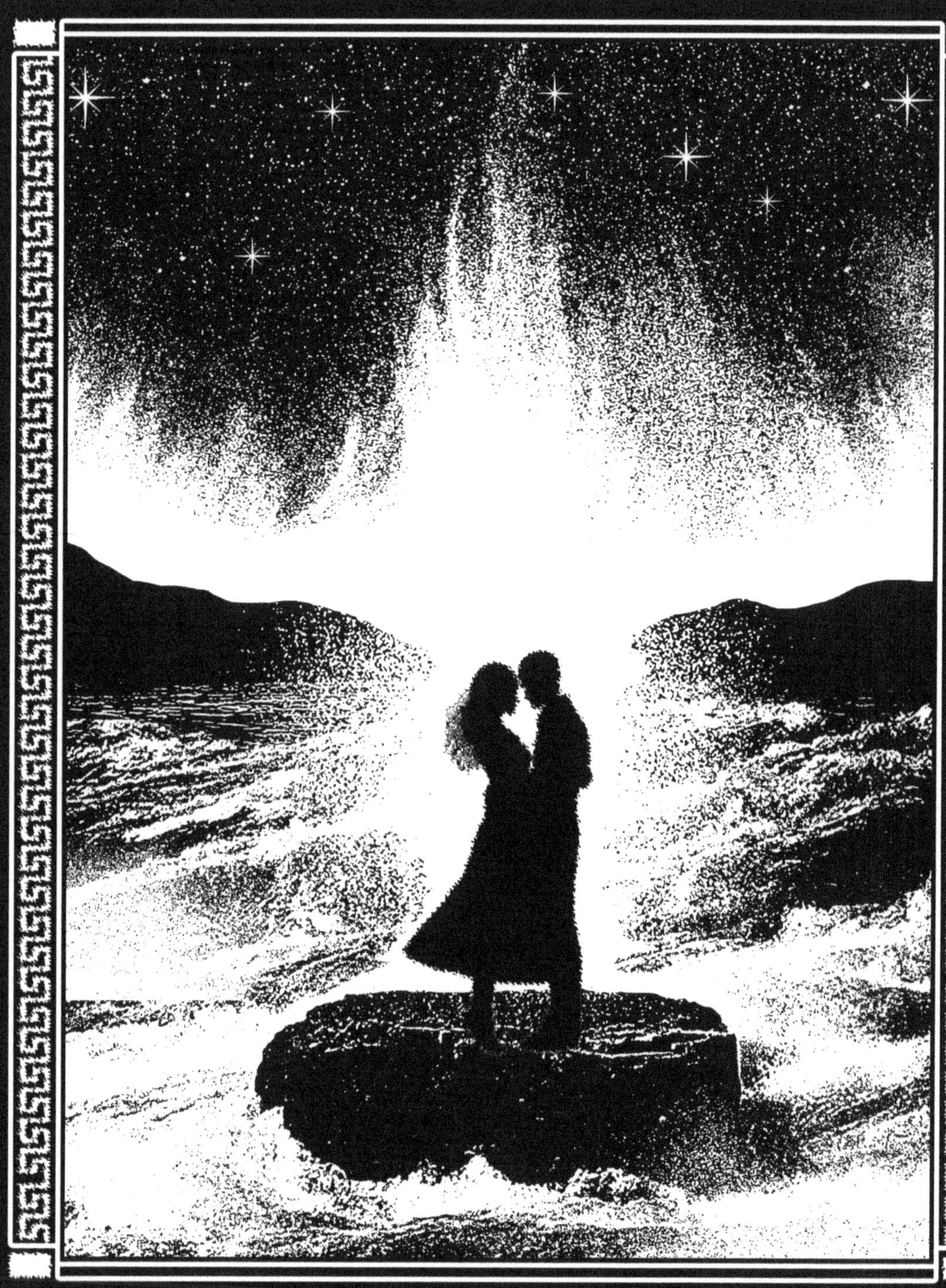

The Fifth Element

Water

Water creates life,
Life created you.
Thirsty, I flow your way,
The nourishing power of you.

Earth

You walk this Earth,
An angel amongst the dirt.
Am I worthy,
Worthy to plant my seeds,
Sow into your fertile Earthly soil?

Wind

Flowing elegantly in the wind,
Your dance hypnotizes me,
A storm that stirs up my soul.
I'll spend my life,
Breathing you in.

Fire

Passion burns bright in our fire,
An inferno that is you.
Incinerate me to ash eternally,
I'll sacrifice my life,
Engulfed in your fiery splendor.

The Fifth Element

The culmination of these elements-
You brought into my life a light profound.

I devote to you:
My flesh and bones

Blood, sweat, and tears.
Water. Earth. Wind. Fire.

The Elements alone-
Not enough.
Lacking one-
Love.

The sparks shine bright,
At the touch of our lips,
A true love's kiss.

I swear this,
My perfect Leeloo:
I belong to you.

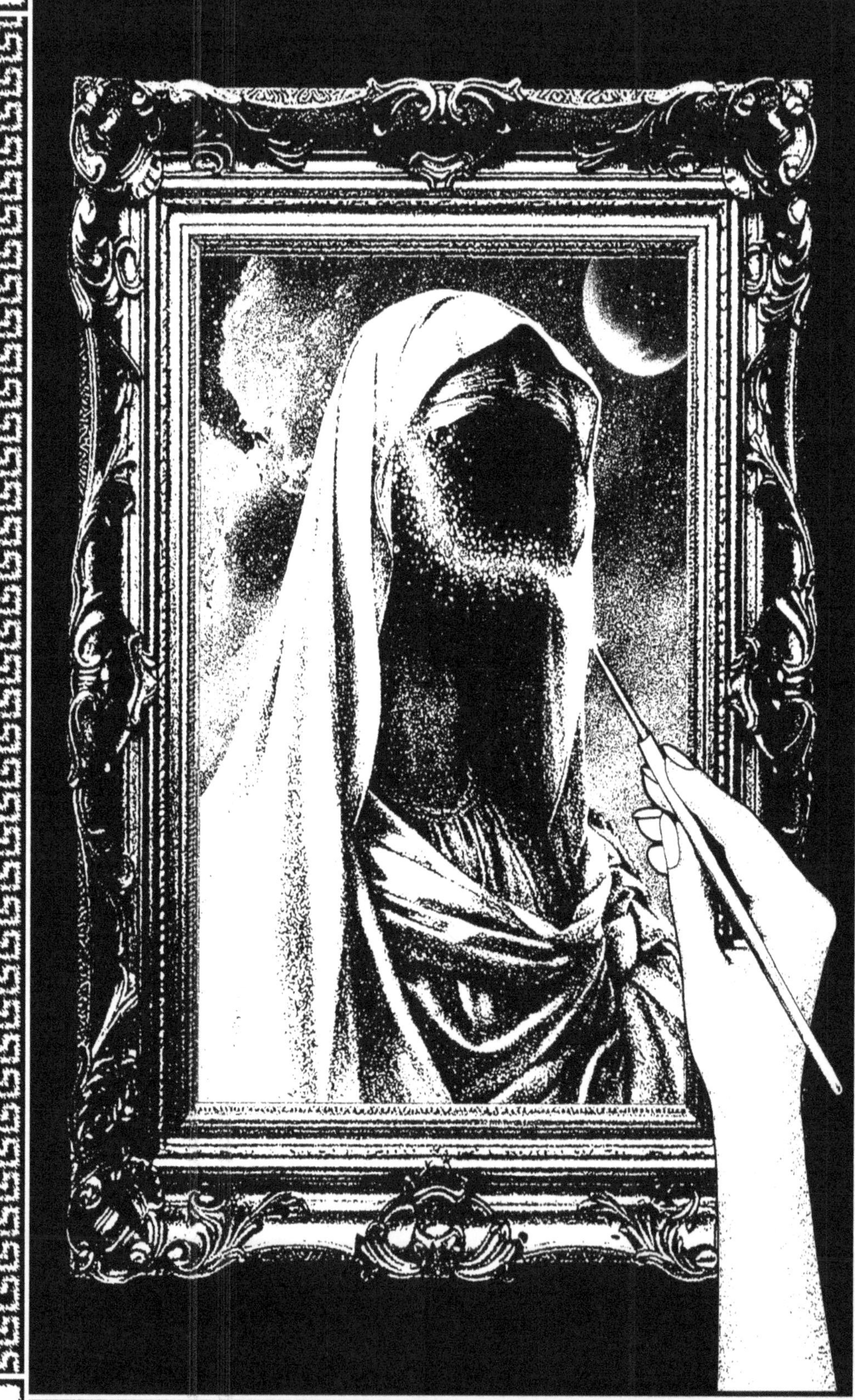

The Artist

The falling of grains of time that fill the empty void of our lives,
Who would have thought that your luminous beauty would have
graced my eyes.

Your acceptance and reciprocation flourished this life to bloom onto
this white, tattered, eternal canvas;
An unrecognizable Fresco

Not even I know the technique and style of which you so elegantly
paint and draw.
You, so humbly state that you are no artist yet here you are, brushing
away.

My darkest black has begun to gray.

Down in the depths of the blackest, oily, mucky, decrepit, crag;
The faintest light shines through the suffering.
The boulders on my broken, bleeding, raw shoulders have softened.
Chains, shackled around my heart, loosened.

I can't imagine an existence now where you are not a part of mine.

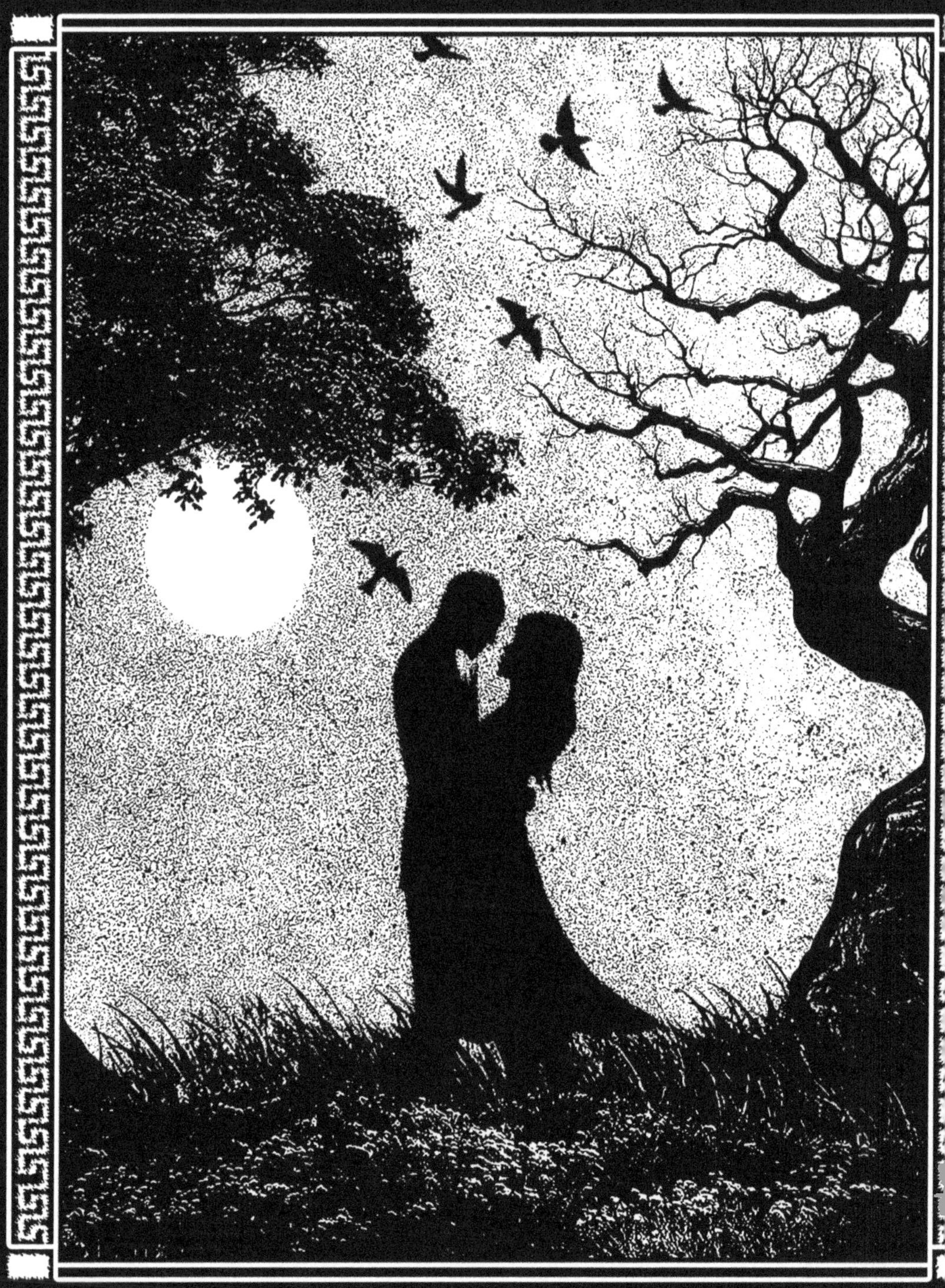

Desire

Seeing you so elegantly walk through the wind,
Hair bristling, flowing; mesmerizing.
Hugging you,
Your scent fills the nose,
My Desire Grows.

Feeling your soft skin on my fingertips,
My urge to trace every curve.
Delicately-
Gently-
Brushing-
Stroking-
Your Desire Grows.

Staring into each other's eyes,
Your sweet Sirens Melody,
My Sharpened Tune.
Convincing both our hearts,
Unveiling all our
Deep,
Dark,
Thoughts.

It's so easy to get lost,
In the waves of
The Brown and the Blue.

Anchored by magnetic pull
Of our lips,
What would it feel like
After all this time?

Soft, succulent,
I bet you taste delicious.
My heart pounds,

As My Desire Grows.
Holding you close,
Closer to my soul.
Feeling each other's …
Well, you know…

…

An inhale,
A gasp.
Our Desire grows.

Hearts pounding,
Tongues lashing.
A bite, a slap,
A nibble, a throw.

Center stage in
The Theater of the Mind,
Yes-
Our Desires grow.

23

Chapter 2: Descent

The single commandment disobeyed,
We are cast out of the promised land.
Our descent into darkness…
Begins…

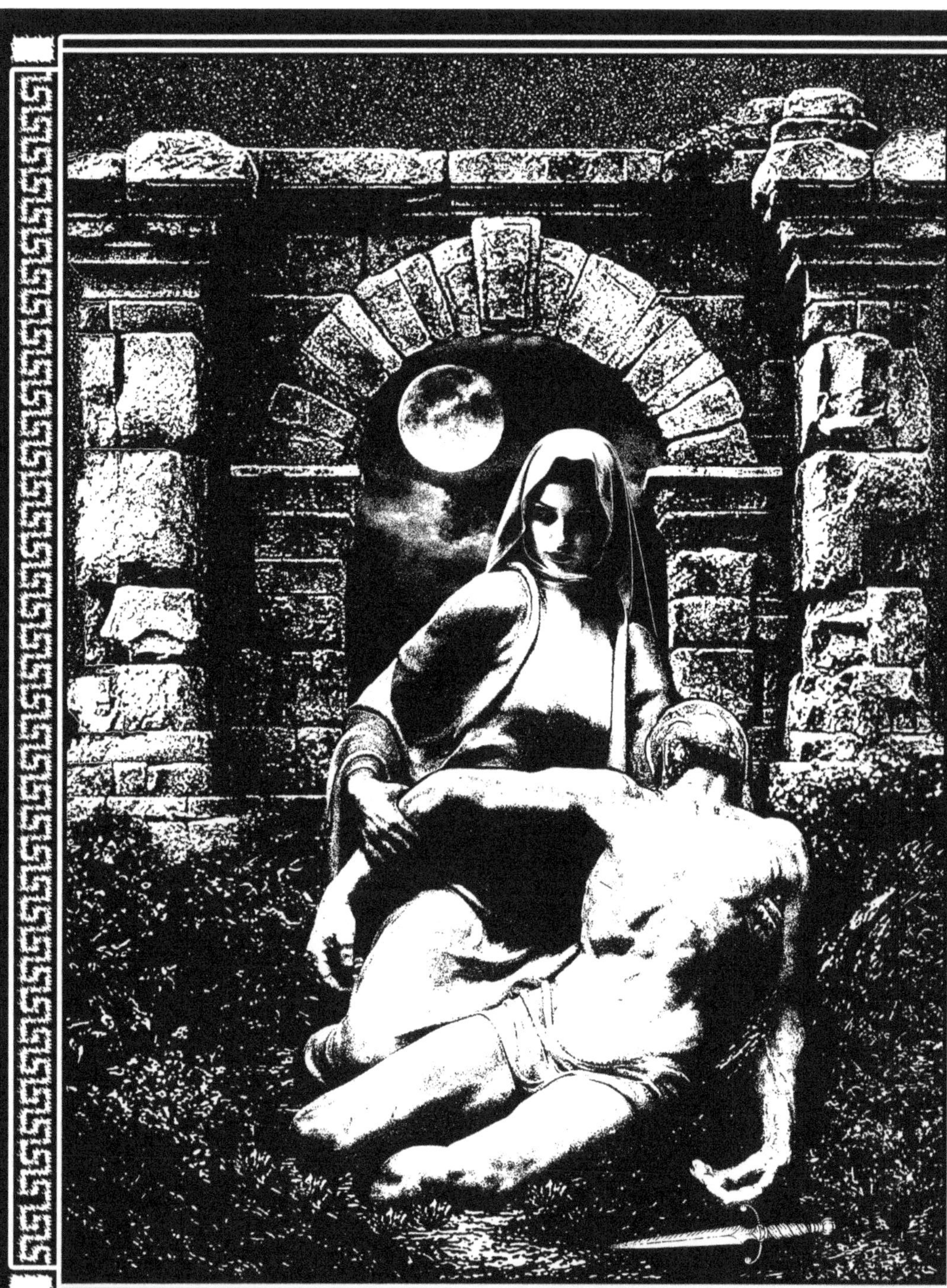

The Taste of Death

Lost in the cold and desolate world.
A figure - alive and warm - graces my aura.
Ever-black flowing hair,
lilac on the nose,
Freckled face,
And brown eyes ensnared my heart that day.

Who are you?

Finding you besides time's great design,
Reluctantly so-you invite me into your court,
Yet pushed away just before our hearts embrace,
Not even a name to be whispered into my aching ears.

Starting again.
And again,
Sacrificing.
Over and over.
These trials,
My first Death-

Restarting from Zero,
Beginning our courtship anew.
I know what's coming:
More death. More suffering.
But all of this,
I'll suffer for you.

Stab me.
Punch me.
Bite me.
Kill me.
I'll endure a million deaths before I give up on you.

My devoured body.
My headless corpse.
My mind shatters - for your protection.

Why won't you love me?

Still, the name I die for goes unspoken.
A final breath whispered from an angel's lips.
The sweet softness of your boney kiss…

Finally, after all this time,
The Taste of Death

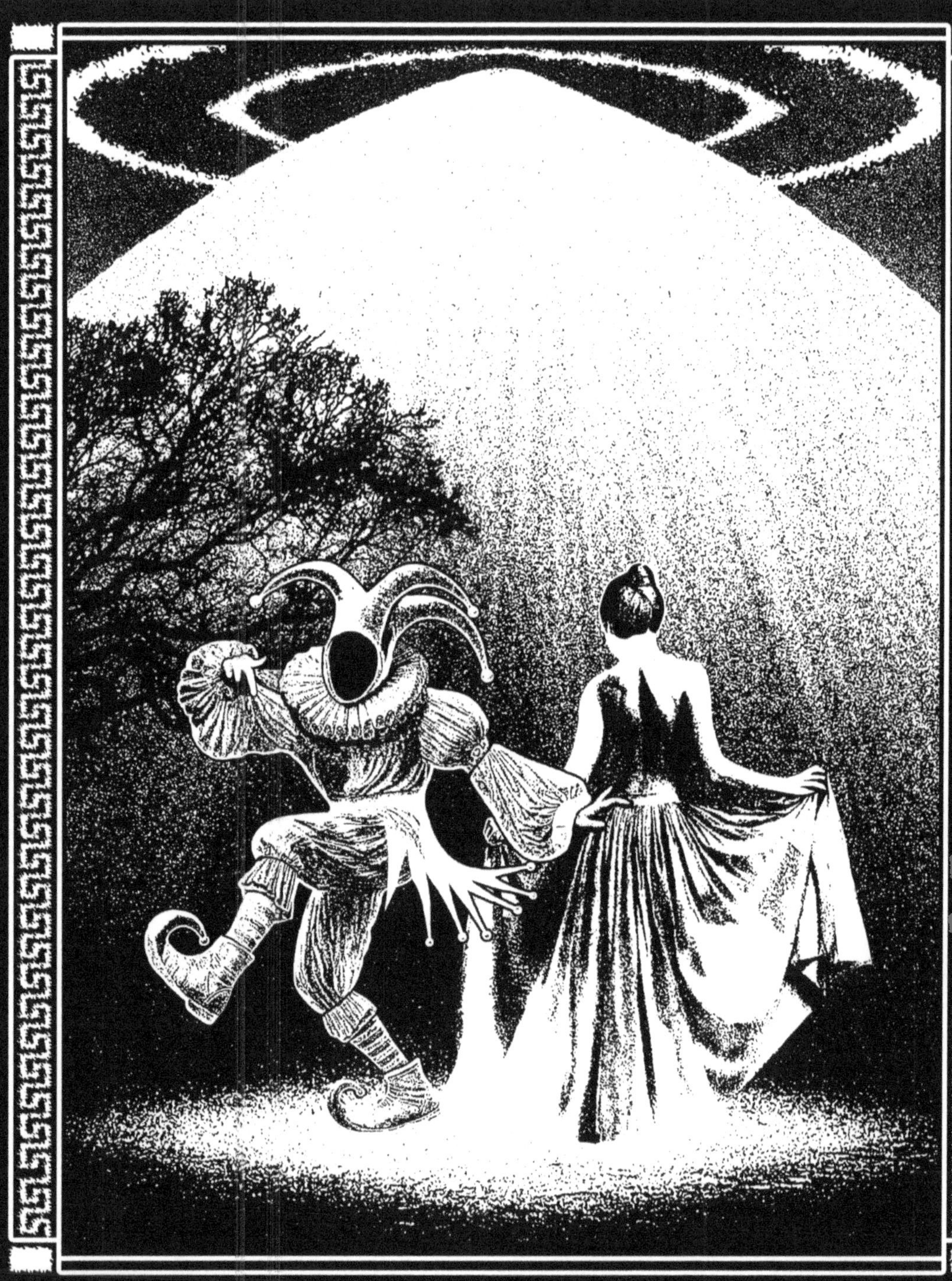

The Jesters Tango

The red and yellow colors of my leather jump suit I don too frequently sting when I run and perform my jester's routine.

The jingle of the bells as I jump and twirl my lovers dance are stark reminders of the joke I'll never understand.

Painting my jesters face black and white, I know deep down my show is not so bleak;
My quarrel with my Master, Pain, I suffer endlessly.

Far too often do I escape my Master's Court - I yearn and forget the affliction I endured,
I dance back to the entrapment of a lover's embrace once more.

My spirit is numb to the tears shed from the song my heart was dancing to.
Still so blissfully I wish to be a jester in your lover's tune.

"The Fool can rise to be The Hero" I state so boldly to your broken and conditioned heart.
I misjudged the thickness from which your scars have formed.

My signature dance, "The Jesters Tango" could not sway or break away your Lover's chiseled stone.

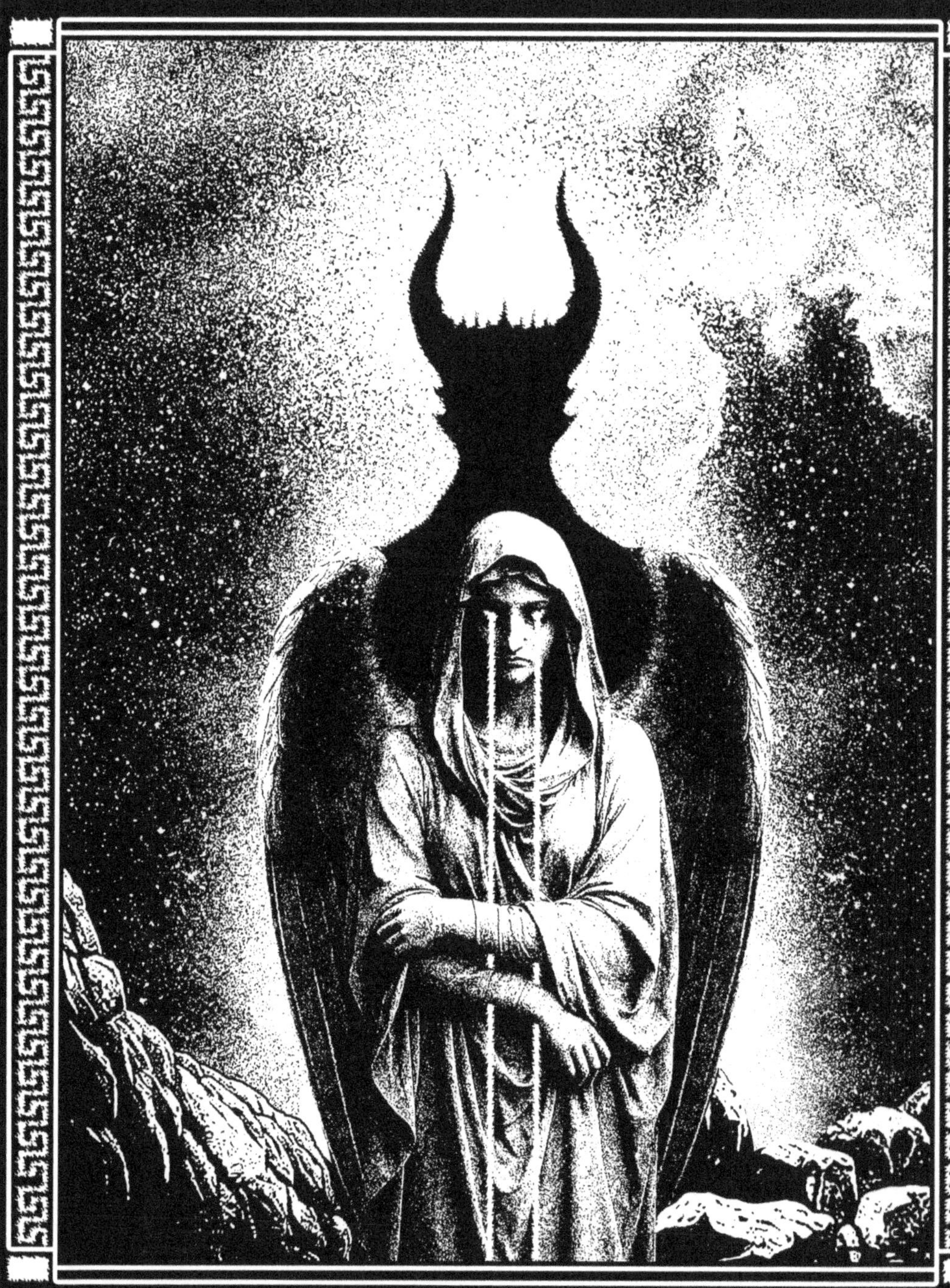

Possession

I can feel you crawling around up there,
In my mind's dusty, decrepit attic.
Skittering your false memories all over the floor,
While crawling on all four.

Slithering your lies through the anthologies that were so beautifully
stored,
The black ichor oozing and slopping from your diseased, putrid lips
onto the tapestry of what was supposed to be,
Soiled and tainted,
As the person I believed you were.

The deaf tones you screech fill the darkness of the room.
No control over your contorted body,
You destroy your very flesh to soothe the demons that have pos-
sessed you.

We're in the 9th layer of hell now,
Your realm of ice and betrayal,
So fitting for one so ironic.
But what is this?

With trumpets and Cherubs of Hell playing as the Revelation is
self-discovered,
In the center of the icy prison,
That beautiful, prideful angel—
The great liar and deceiver.

Lucifer…

That is your name.

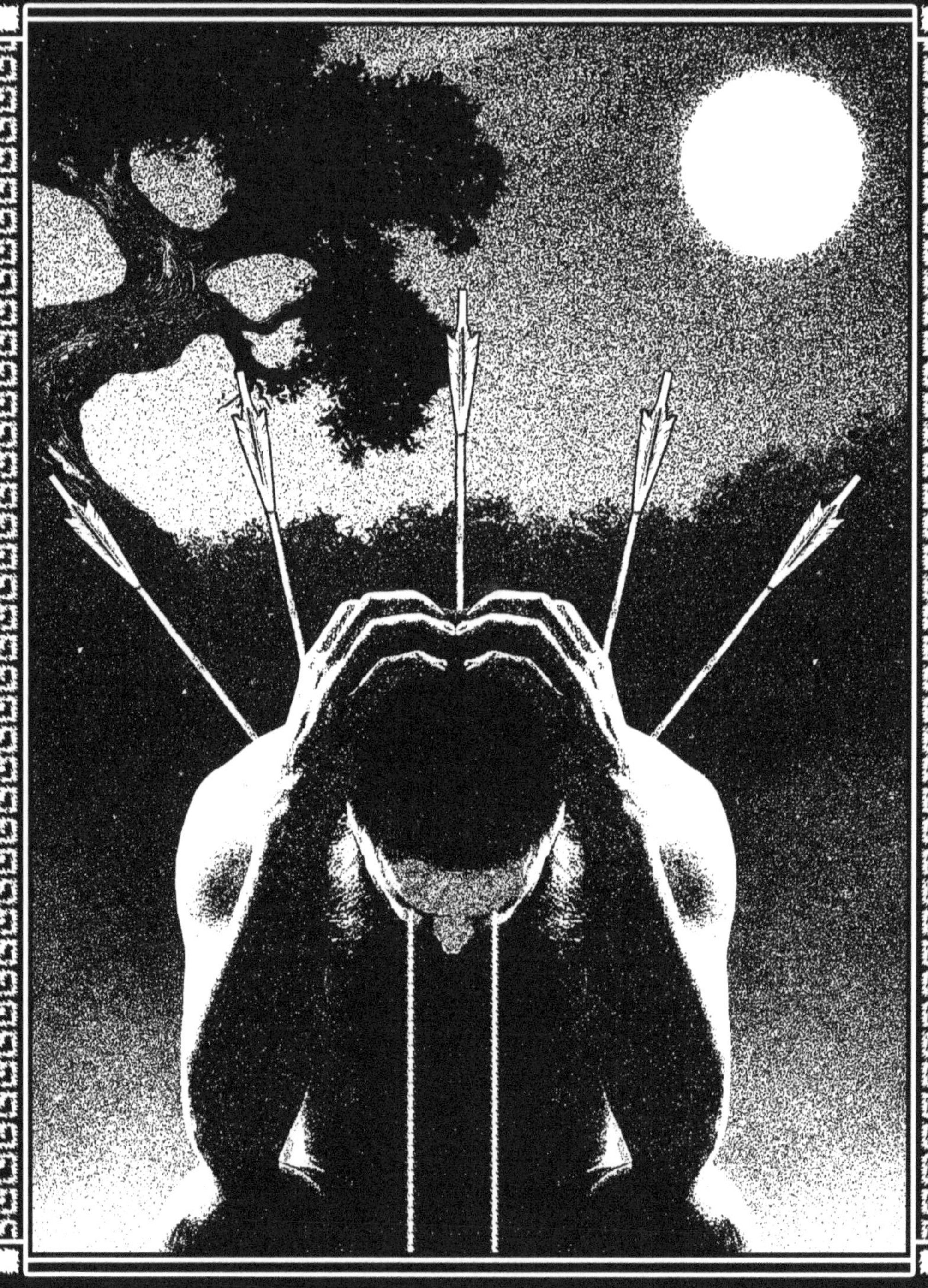

Pain

I'm in so much pain.
So much excruciating mental anguish that my body recognizes this
as physical pain.
The pit of my stomach turns as anxiety sets in.
The low hum keeping me on edge.

I reach out to my "friends" to hopefully have an outlet to release
some of this pressure that's boiling over, yet all I'm met with is
silence.
I'm met with the too busy'"'s.

I have nowhere to turn to except inward.
I have to internalize the pain and keep on going.

Nobody cares.

I'm a Man.

I know this will eventually subside but my God this is excruciating.
I wish I could cry and let all the pain out.
The light from my eyes is noticeably gone.

What would life be if not for pain.

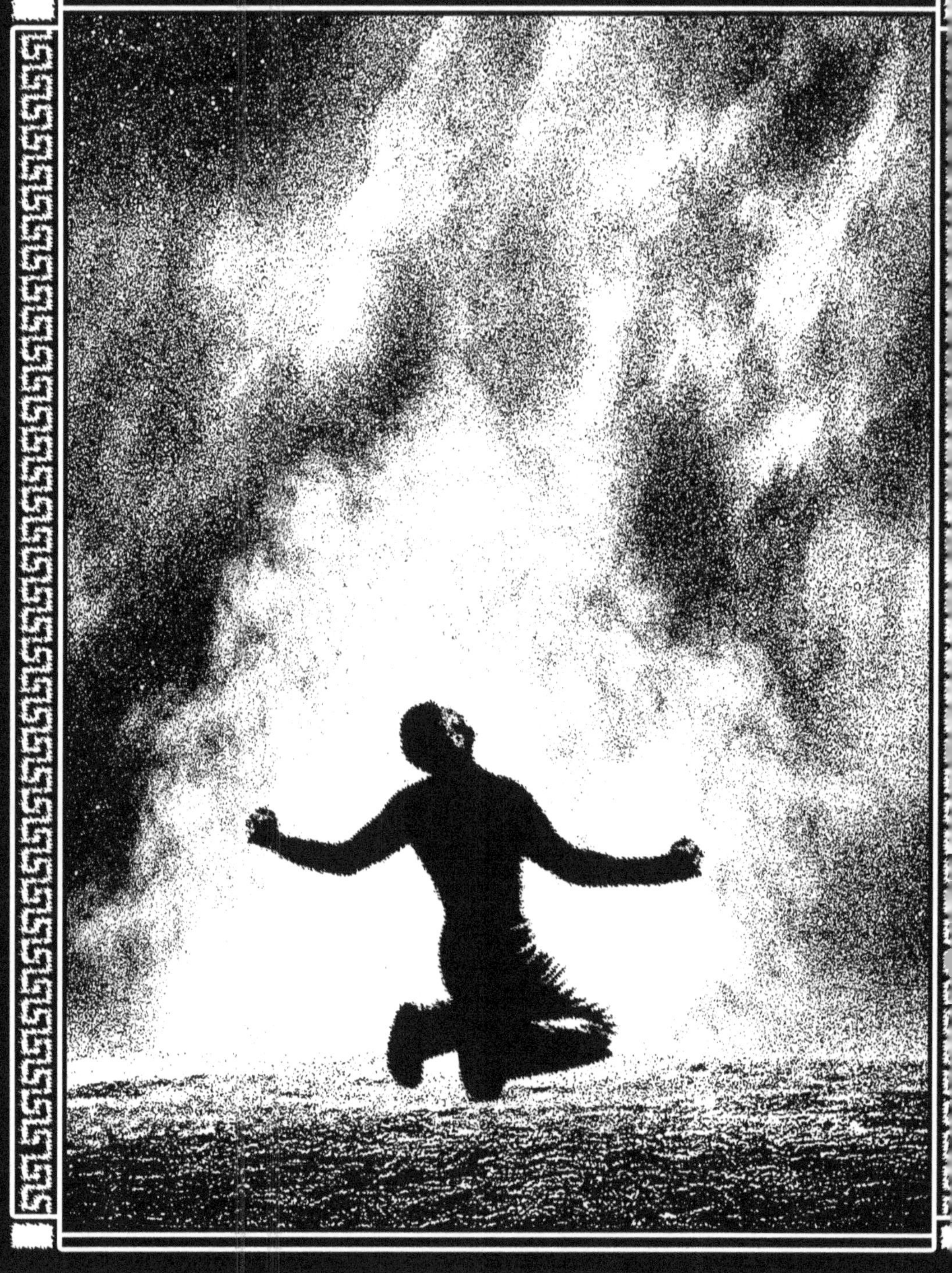

Rage

This raging inferno inside me incinerates all.
My suppression system is all but depleted.
It can only hold the anger until I'm boiling over.

My tears quench this intense heat.
These flames are insatiable.

I'm compressed into this immense gravity.
Imploding on myself whenever my mind wanders.
There needs to be a flood of emotion to release this pressure.

This ocean is sizzling.
My rage is eternal.
I am eternal.
My pain is forever.
My pain… is an illusion.

I'm boiling over.
Not an external destruction.
I'm a self-destructive nuclear bomb.
Incinerating all my progress.

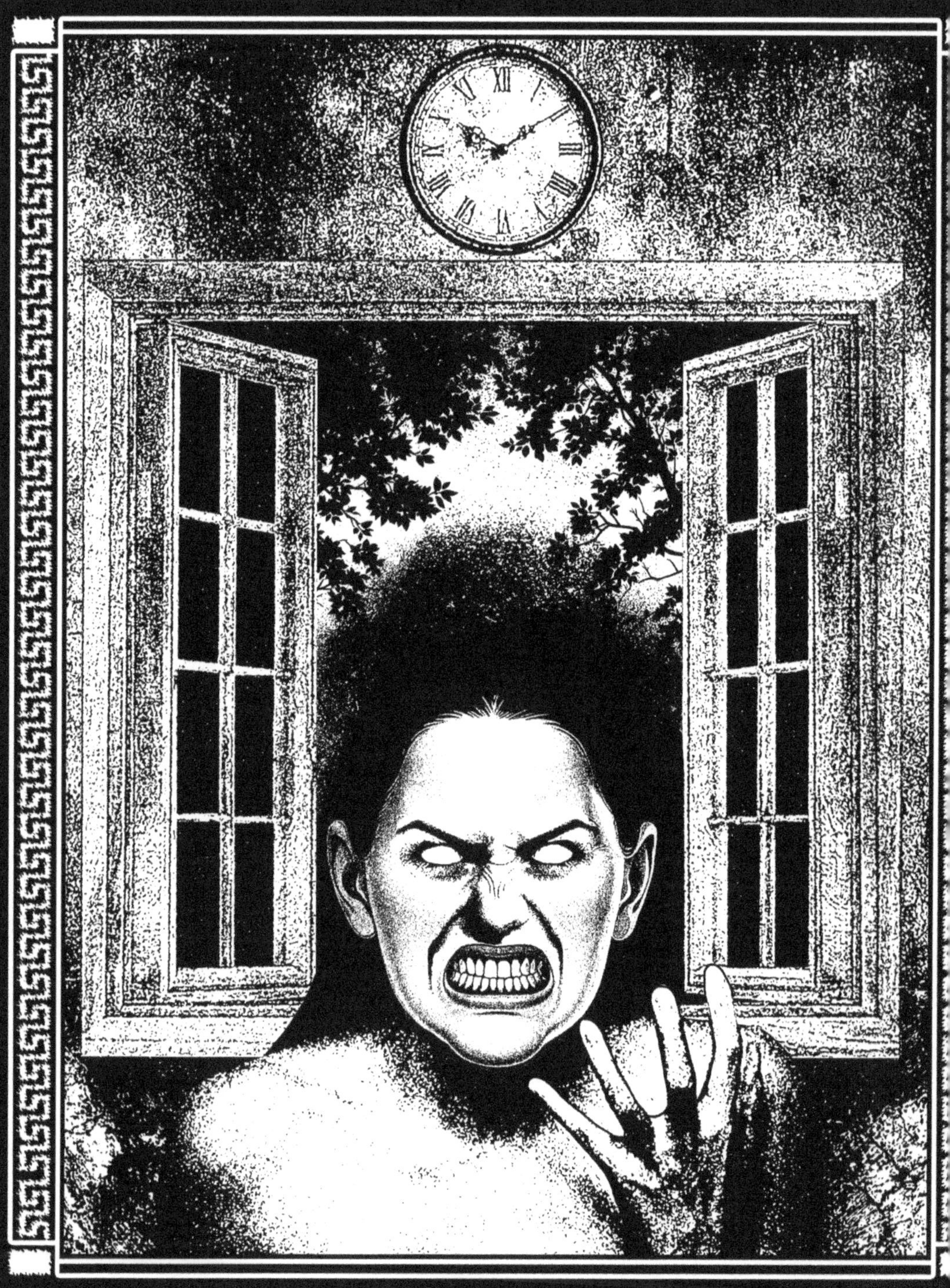

Gritted Teeth

Another wake up, another bright sunny day,
I'll grit my teeth once more and confront it with rage.
There is so much pain inside of me,
It's bursting at the seams.

The machine is churning and the cog must spin,
There's no rest for the wicked in me.
The soul of this machine was promised,
Yet now found - empty just as me.

Gritted teeth, I must push on.
Realities blend truth with lies.
No aid coming,
Even with signal flares high in the sky.

Tears burst through the windows of my soul,
Releasing built up pressure.
Anger takes its place,
Better than the sadness seeping back in.

Gritted teeth, I must push on.
Unable to explain the voices inside my head,
The sweet angelic call I hear breaking my silent screams,
With promises of peace, of clarity…
No, wait.
It's sadness attempting to latch its claws back in.

With Gritted Teeth,
I will stop the cycle
of this
Spiraling Machine.

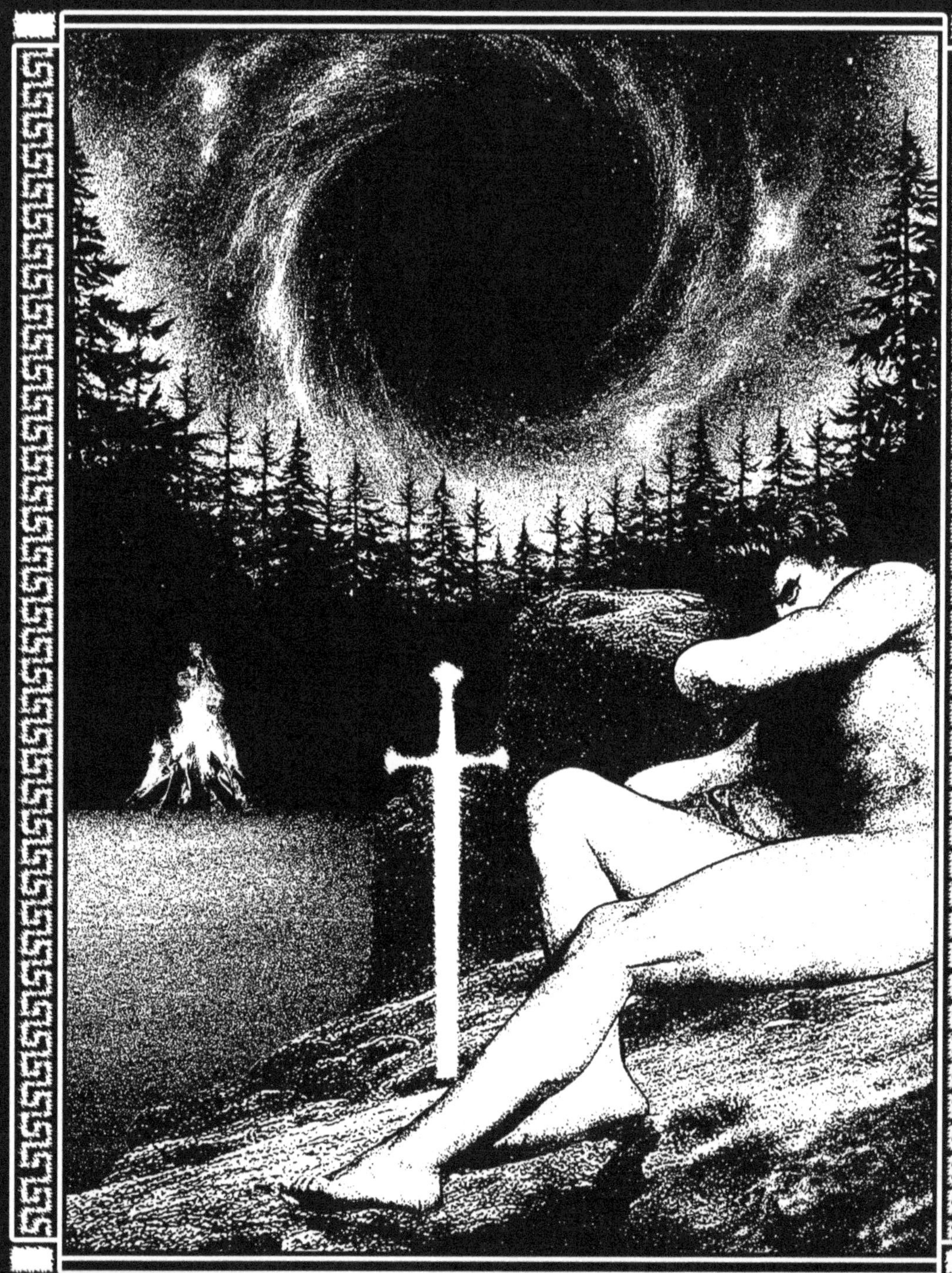

Respite

Sprinting in this forest of life.
Battling the demons of my past,
Denying the maw of death,
So eagerly open for me.

Fighting on the battlefield of my youth,
Alone,
My valor swayed.

My armor is rusted,
My blade is dull.
I'm tired of walking-
The weight of it all.

I need someone to give me permission to break.

Respite…
A bonfire nearby.
Resting my weary bones from life's missteps,
Its travels.
Here, in the heat of the flame,
It burns away the freeze of my entropy.

Caressing my hardened spirit through the windows of my soul,
The warmth rejuvenates.

I can see the screams of my past in the flame's crackling, snapping,
life.

I cannot show weakness,
Everyone is watching.
But deep down,
I need to break down.

I need respite from the memories.
I need silence from the pain.
I will push on but….

I am a Man
And I need a break.

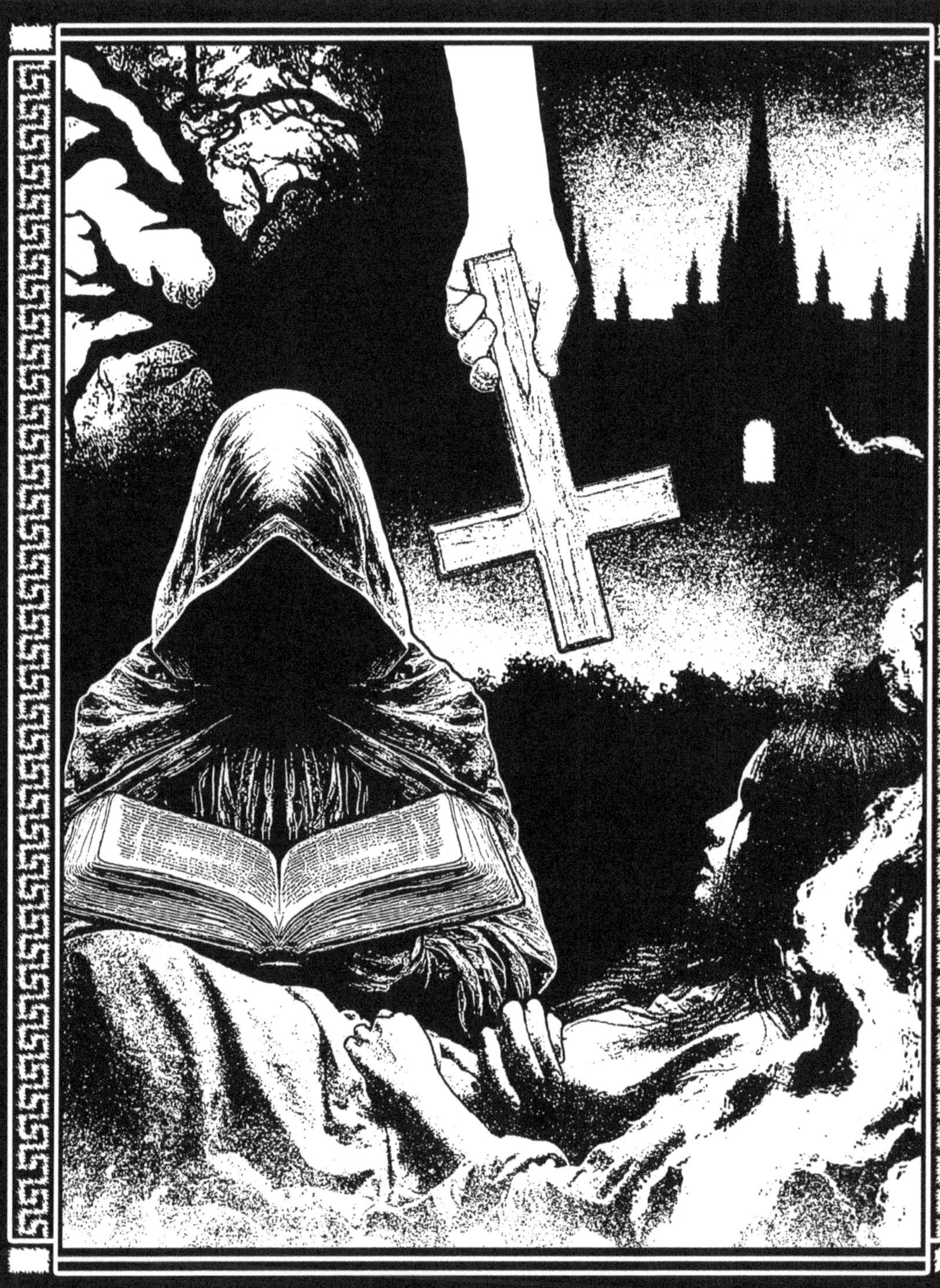

Exorcism

Down in the depths of the everlasting freezing hell of your (my)
betrayal,
I've found my strength to push on and exorcise this demon from you
(me).
The demons have consumed all of you (me),
No meat for the maggots to feast on.

The occult ritual requires my (your) blood and flesh to separate
the soul sucking Pazuzu from your fragile and weak spirit.
The name, delivered unto my weary mind by an unknown entity.
Forming in the black Void,
The letters of the commander of all Wind Demons.

You (I) will not survive this separation.

Cutting deep into my heart, the most sacred flesh,
Sawing and ripping to get every necessary drop of blood,
Every pound of flesh needed to complete the ritual.

The black candles lit-
A leather-bound book written in human blood,

1. "Liber Infestationis Daemonicae",

Opened.
The words recited-

2. "Vade retro Pazuzu, Adjuro te, spiritus nequissime,
   ut desinas infestare creaturam Dei"

Swirling black ocean of nothingness takes over my essence.
No longer is the permeating cold of this 9th layer obliterating my
body.
I'm plunged deep into a void; the dark yellow eyes of the inhabitants
circle me like sharks.

They smell my wounded soul…
Infestation has set in.

I should have known.
A leather-bound book written in human blood.
The words recited, even if holy, are tainted by evil.

Your Exorcism was my Possession.

Translation for "Exorcism (Latin):
1."The Book of Demonic Infestation."
2."Go back, Pazuzu. I adjure you, most wicked spirit, to cease
tormenting this creature of God."

<u>*Authors Note*</u>
For those who are fans of horror movies, you might find that the
Demon in this poem is the same Demon from the Cinematic mas-
terpiece "The Exorcist" (1973). I chose Pazuzu and Latin as Pazuzu
preys on the weak and those easily manipulated. Latin adds a layer
of occult horror that I love to incorporate into my works.

Chapter 3: Abyss

Only in the Abyss can we find ourselves,
The horrors become home.
Maybe we were always here…
Maybe…
They were always munching on our bones.

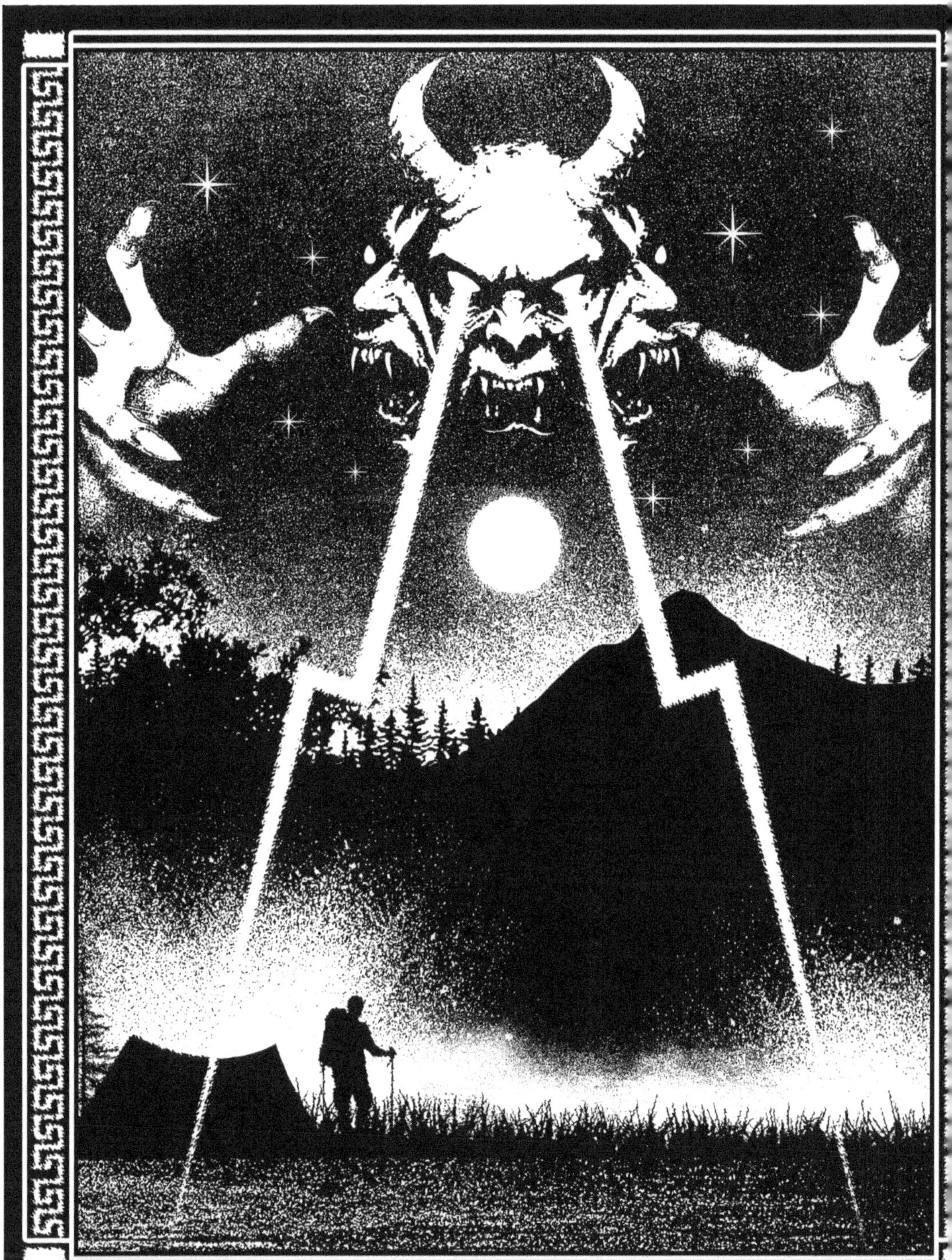

Two-Face

Camping deep in Idyllwild's darkened, mist-veiled forest,
Reports of a haunting creature rise with whispered dread.
Grim accounts of terror-stricken campers,
Mutilated victims laid bare-
Why is this a familiar sight to me?

The rumors of the Two-Faced monster must be true and if this evil exists,
Then so too must exist the soul-banishing power of the Mirror of Reflec-
tion the holds its youth.

Two-Face; Sucking the life force of all who witness its disgust,
It stitches the lies onto its skin.

Arming myself with the knowledge of the creature;
The hidden lore of the Mirror of Reflection-
I step into the blackness of the night.
Hoping to find the Two-Faced Monster to end its blight.

The earth, Pine scented, as the mist rolls off the mountain,
The trees' leaves bristle and whisper their nightly tune - the winds soft
howling,
The haunting has begun to go bump in the night.

Heavy footsteps reverberating across the forest floor-
Shaking everything, from roots to my trembling boots.
Waking the creepy crawlers, critters, and spirits once more.
Snapping twigs, breaking branches, the beast lurches in the dead of night!

Decaying flesh and sin are heavy on my nose,
Blood and death have lifted into the air.
Oppression and evil weigh heavy on my soul.
Its presence-

The hairs on the back of my neck erect!
Heart thundering, I turn and lock eyes with its deep crimson gaze…

Snarling teeth and putrid breath,

Two-Face SCREAMS!

Terrified, I raise the Mirror of legend to let the beast drink in its Reflection.
Louder and louder the screams become,
Ear shattering, brain splattering, I match the screams of Death and see…

In the mirror I stand as he; Two-Face... and it… Me.
"Evil comes in Threes. I may be two faced, but can you defeat the Evil in Thee?"

I (it) flee into the Darkness of Night, swallowed whole by The Forest's might.
Now facing the darkness, I stand alone.
Two-Face; it was more afraid than I.

Maybe…
The monsters really are just *US* in disguise.

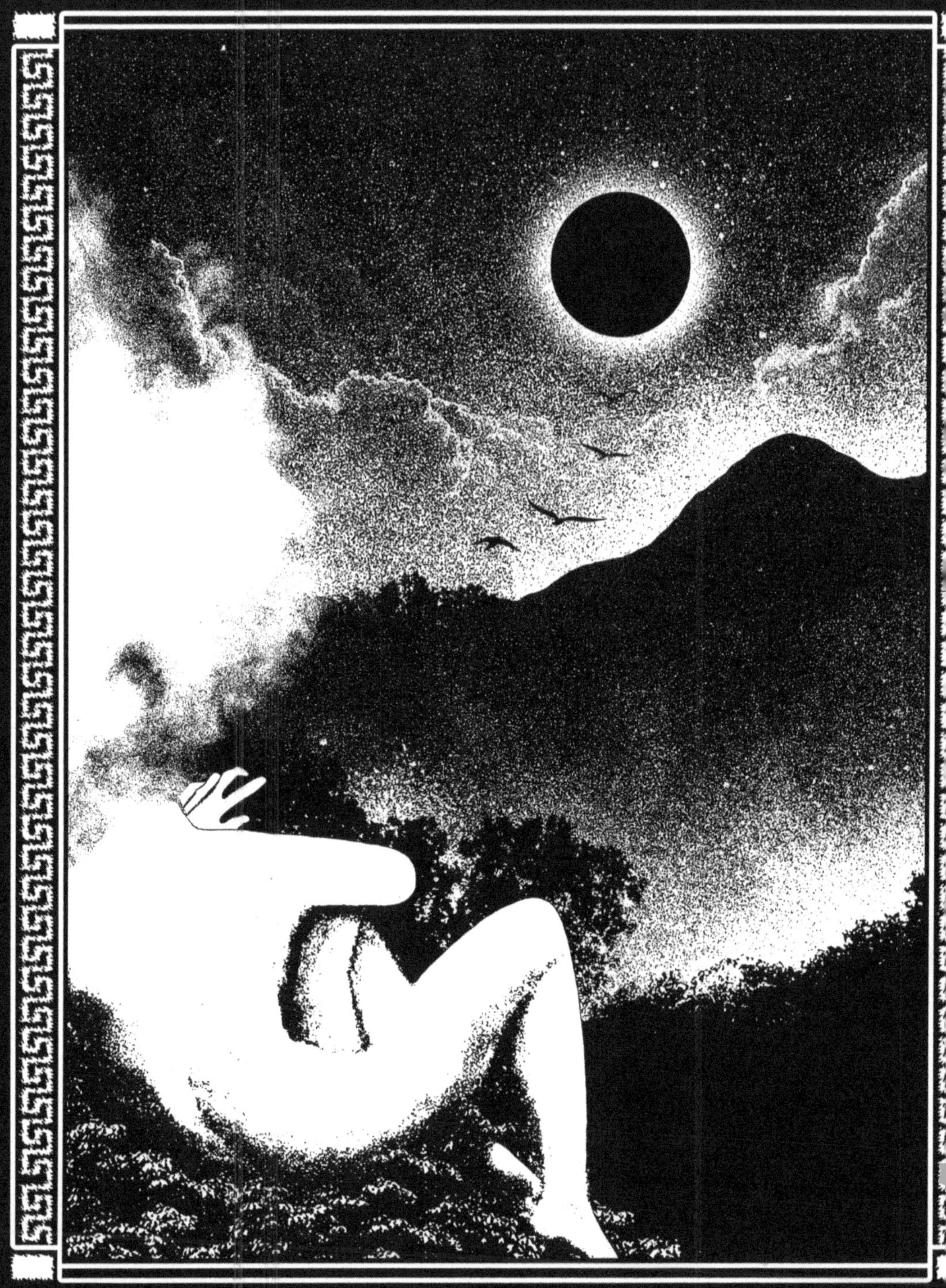

A Dark Place

The dead weight of the past lingers-
narrow, crooked fingers pressing into my aching shoulders.
Arched from carrying the images to the present.

The memories of time spent blissfully in each other's grasp-
In each other's gaze…

This dead weight carries me down into the cold dark depths of Lake
Despair.
The abyss encroaches on me,
Lapping and nipping at my mind.
Flooding its way in…

It's strange how just a tune, a scent, a sight-
Enough to break the dam -
Filling the void with forsaken thoughts.
Pain and suffering yet again water-log my entity.

The memories are not what I miss.
The feeling of those memories…

Endless….

A Dark Place.

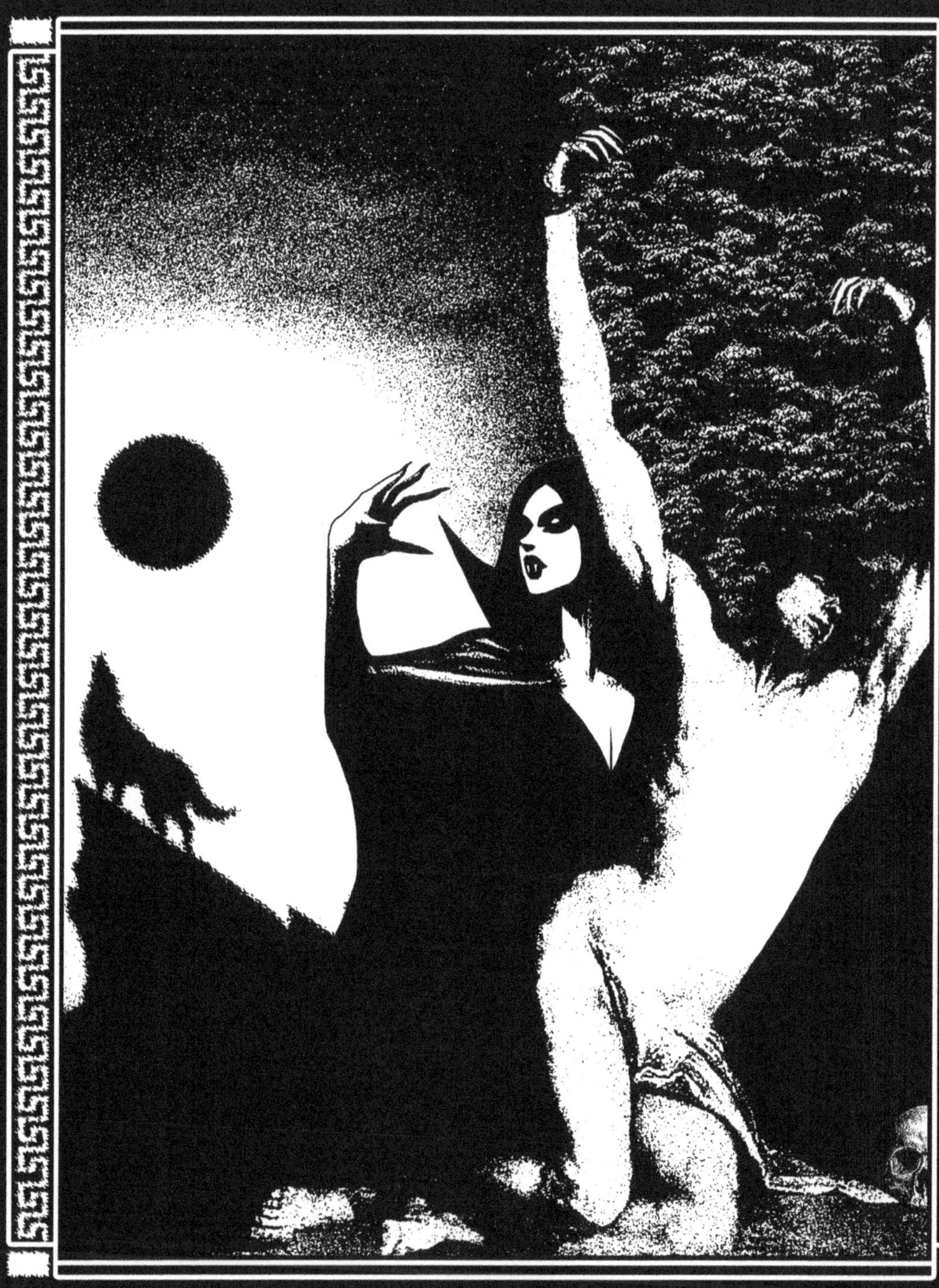

Essence of Humanity

Once upon a time,
As these stories so often begin,
A man destined for greatness.
A Lie.

Trouble and turmoil,
I bared the struggles upon my shoulders.
Strong and mighty my flesh grows,
Yet my heart…
Longing so…

Humanity at its essence,
Perseverance.
The Lie turned to a truth.
Greatness no longer just a thought,
A reality.

Age stalked the man,
A wolf in the blackened night.
The Forest of life,
A hunting ground of might.

This story is not for him.
There is no happy ending.
Just like life,
The man is fragile,
Yet full of compassion.

"What will I be?
When will I go?
I must find my love,
For a Rose to grow."

A withered soul found in the forest.
Is this destiny?

Carried into my cabin,
Invited her in, and with it my sin,
Into my home.

Its scent fills the nose,
Juniper berries, earth, pine.
A withered soul not,
But a woman.

"My thanks to thee, young man,
I've been starving for centuries.
I will reward thee,
Bestow some ancient knowledge."

Her words- strange,
How ancient must she be?
Intrigued, I wonder-
Does she know what ails me?

What's that in the air?
Scent of blood, thick with malice,
Heavy as the night.
Death, the stalker, lingers near.

"A secret long kept,
Come hither to me,
I whisper the answer to aging-
Your deepest fear."

Now close,
Hypnotized.
She bites down,
Drawing deep.

Kissing on my neck,
Seduction as we speak.

Humanity's essence,
Once sacred and in me,
Now flowing freely.
Fear, Excitement, Ecstasy.
My Love,
She has found me.

Crimson hot- burning,
Gushing into the gaping maw of the lapping,
Impatient woman.
She did say she was starving…

My heart fading…
My life at her lips…

"A Gift for you", she whispers angelically,
Her lips brushing mine.
"Eternity."

A withered soul no more,
A Vampiric Mistress,
Transformed.

Even with my fireplace lit and kindling,
The warmth is sapped and sucked from the room.
Freezing death is here,
At the bedroom door,
Gleaming Obsidian,
Staring.

The Stars and Universe in her eyes.
The darkest,
Most beautiful,
even in the night.

Whisked away.
Death and I,
Now One.
My Loving Master,
Draped in her crimson,
velvet dress.
Fiery red hair,
Pale skin,
Purple lipstick-

The perfect flower.
My Rose.

She drunk me dry this night,
My fears now gone.
Death is her name.
She sings me lullabies with grace.

Essence of Humanity,
She smelled it in me.
Now hers Eternal,
Vampirically Enthralled.

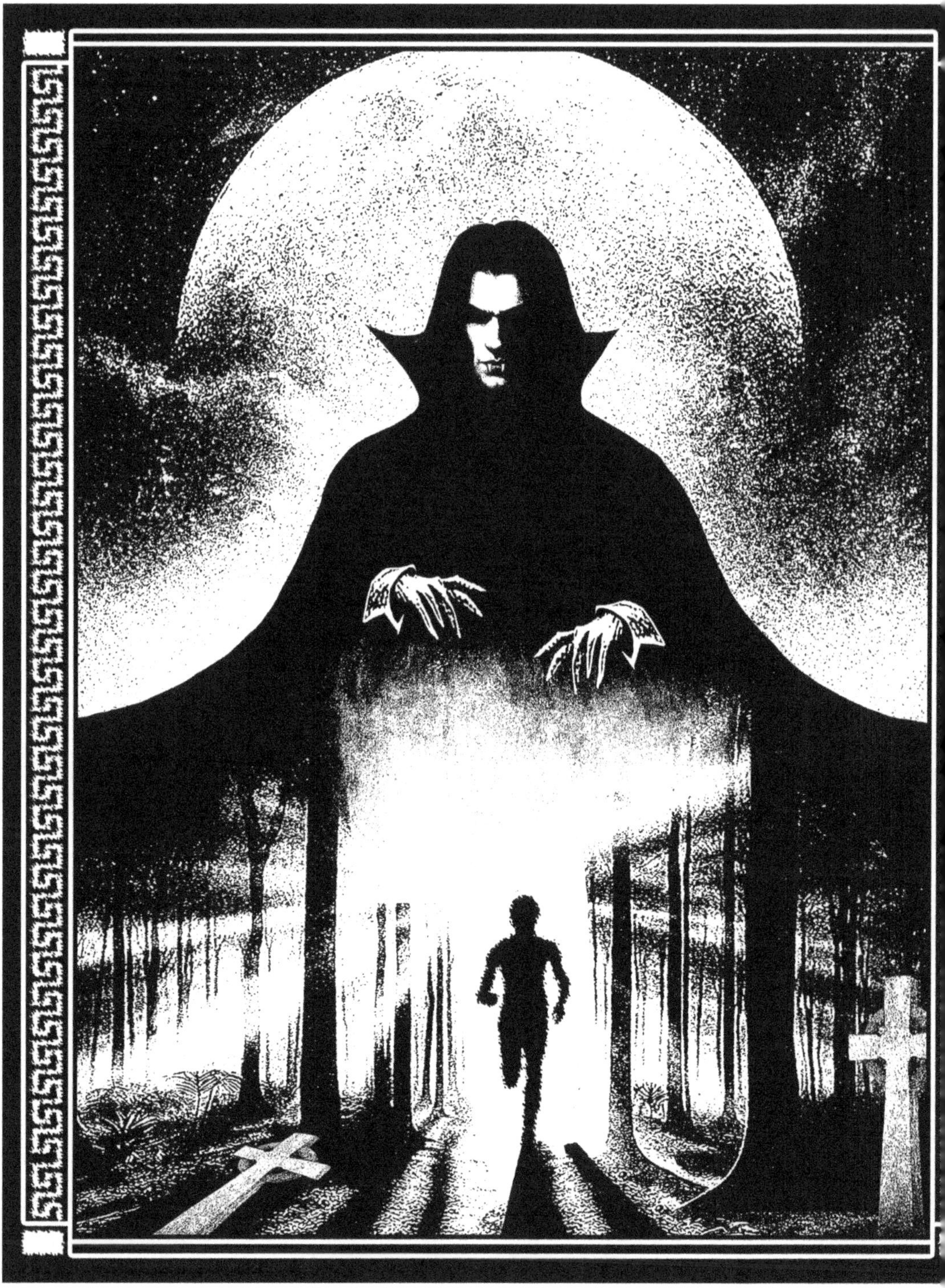

Death

Silvered moonlight bathes the cold forest night,
Chill rolls onto the earthy ground.
Fearing the night hunter approaching,
Life hides away deep into their dens.

Stalking the succulent and tender flesh of the lost,
This Forest is home to Death.
Or at least that's the name the forest creatures have given it,
The monstrosity that stalks the night - a Vampire.

Stealing the life through their veins,
Death spares none in the moonlight of night.
Beautifully - Sucking the scarlet into him.
This Vampire now free from its Masters bond.

"I am no longer Me…
Now just an everlasting Death for thee…
My Rose - my Master…
Abandoned me to eternally roam the Forest."

Another creature of this land dried,
Not enough to satiate the lust burning in the fiery blackened heart.
A desire burning enough to escape the confines of sanity,
A bloodlust frenzy encapsulates…

The hunted - Fair skinned maiden,
Wandering into the mystery of the forest.
An eternal gravesite,
Unbeknownst to her.

Stalking the prey in the stillness of the night,
Yes, every step you take - I will see my way into you tonight.

"I am Death and this is my Forest.
An eternal prison - your new home.
Join me in the night, my new found prey,
Fair maiden - death is just a suck away."

My Darkness spreads expansively,
Gliding down to the shocked lamb.
Unwillingly taken to their grave,
My new eternal mate.

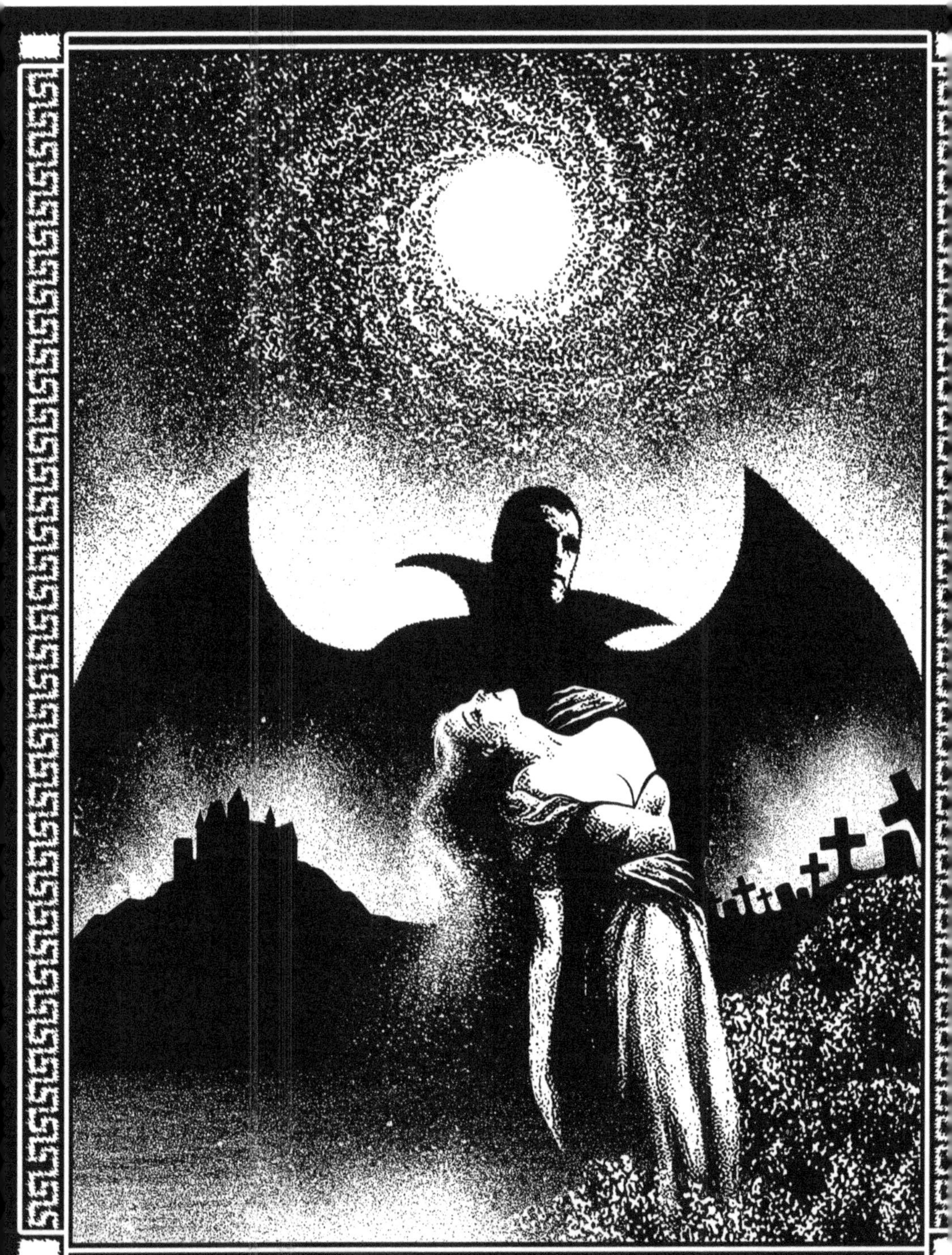

Hypnosis

The Moon hangs high in the night,
Yes, the cool air rises.
I spread my shadow draped wings,
With blood starved eyes-
My brown-eyed prize.

Swooping silently,
The celestial sky sings.
What a haunting tune rings,
In between my midnight wings.

We lock eyes,
My brown stars fall into your hazel honey.
Your words reject,
Yet your eyes ensnare,
Inviting me in.

Hypnotized by my gaze,
The vampiric hunger will satiate.

A fracture in time,
A spell cast in wait.

The scent of your blood-
I breathe you in.
Our noses dance together-
Forbidden fruit tasted,
Sweetness that transcends time.

Soft and warm,
Electric and ecstatic.
A fleeting memory,
But our lips will remember.

The spell deepens,

Threads unseen tighten,
You are mine tonight,
My delicate prey.

My nature calls,
SHARP.
A bite,
A gasp,
A shuddering pull,
Ecstasy spilling, crimson warmth running,
Your heartbeat thrumming beneath my lips.
I bury myself in your pleasure.

Pulling you close,
One taste, and I'll drink you whole.

The deliciousness of you-
It drives me merry.

The crimson steaming,
But your honeyed eyes freeze my fire.
What is this?

I'm hypnotized by you.

My desire burns unquenched,
A hunger throbbing but restrained.
You tease me so-
Afraid of a passion beyond control?

Ravenous-
Vampiric-
The Queen of Me,
I am bound by the threads of your Witch's spell.

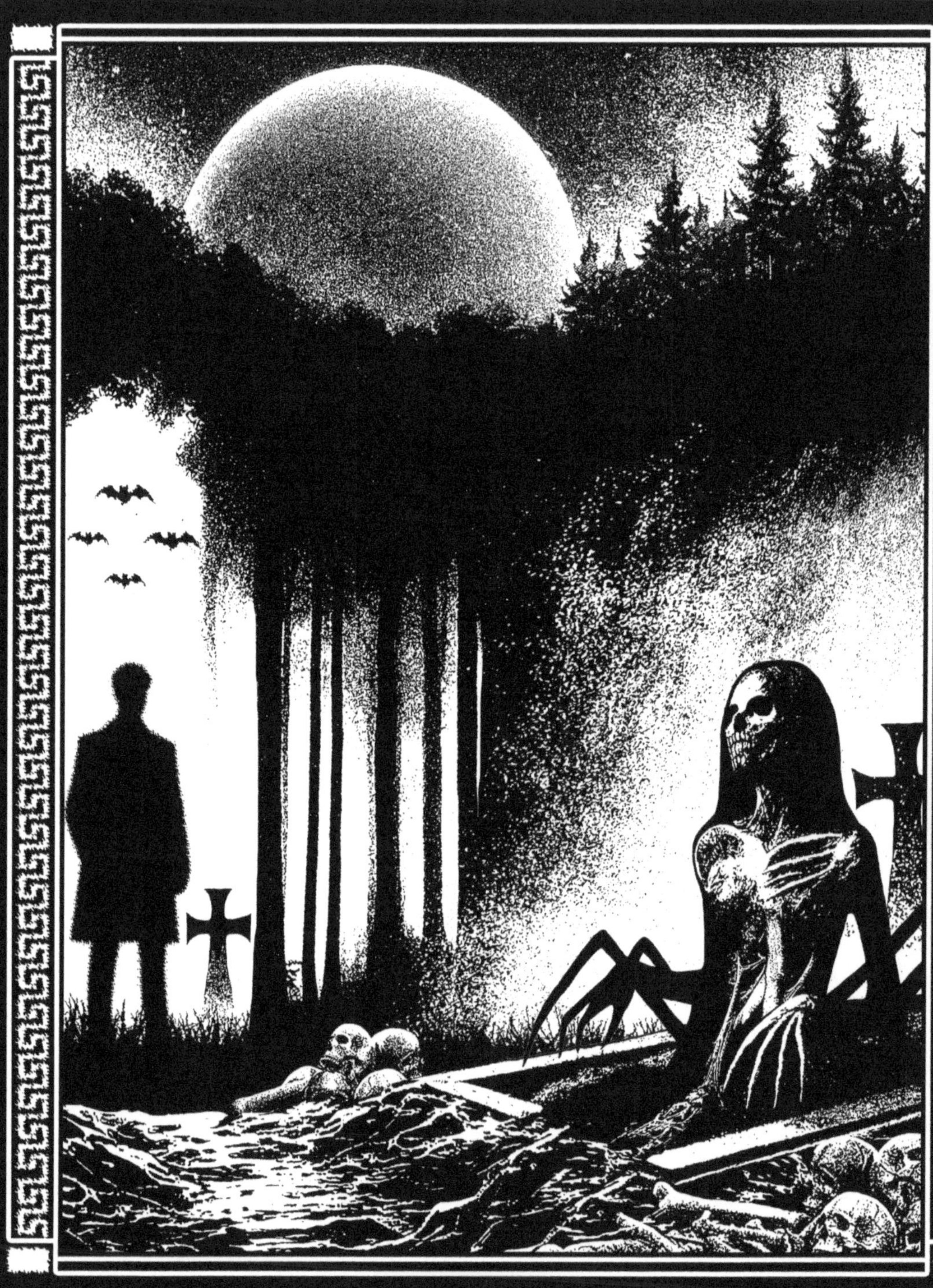

Skin Walker

I looked at her grave as I was standing over it.
Solemnly in my heart I mourned,
Wishing this reality was not mine.

Death finally took her,
Or at least a form of death,
She is no longer mine.

Deep down in the recesses of my spirit,
I feel the pull of her angst.
Her hate for me is palpable.
My letdown is unbearable.

The crawlers are feasting on my beloved's corpse now.
Returned to the earth as we all do,
How I wish to rot with her.

Her ghastly moan-
I can almost feel her icy grip piercing my visage.
The discontent with who I am.

The creatures from beyond the grave have feasted on my face.
I'm but a shambling thing now.
Nothing for even the bugs to eat.

I turned around and saw her once more.

My love…
My life…

Terror came over me.

She spoke to me in an angel's voice,
So sweet and violent,
Anger and lust.

She whispered to me our sweet nothings.

Her eyes - black and deep - as the void I'm trapped in.
Her lips: rigid, slender, arachnid chelicerae to pull me in.
Her teeth sink into me.
Such love and compassion she shows as she crunches on my bones.

Marrow flows freely for her.
The joy in her soulless gaze.
My warmth,
My essence being swallowed up.

This beautiful lie wearing her skin,
It was always wearing her skin.

It was never her…

It was always…
Wearing her skin.

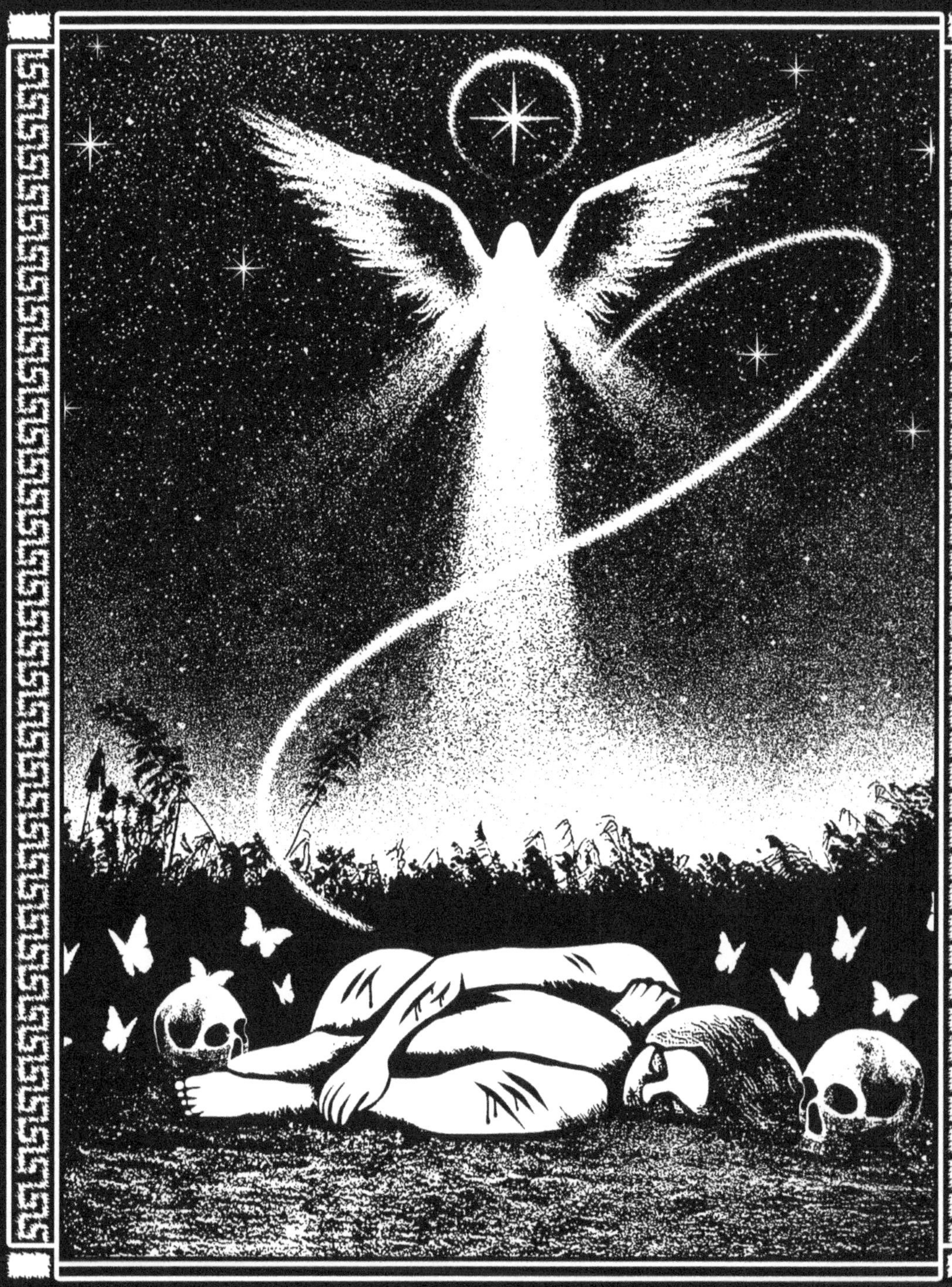

A Penance Unpaid

One Lashing,
And the sting returns to my flesh.
The familiar whip cracks its hardened, leathery knot against my
softened skin-
Breaking it, letting the blood flow.
The Penance paid today is for yesterday's rage.

Two Lashings,
Another CRACK across my back.
The pain suffered released matches the debt owed,
The Scorned Lovers hushed demand,
Penance owed for Yesterday's Lie

Three Lashings,
Whipping intensifies and the scars deepen.
My horror emerges, consuming me,
The Darkness within is kept at bay.

Four Lashings,
Dark aid guiding my trembling hands.
The Devil himself arises from the shadowy corners of this Chapel,
laying his Cindered hand on my head.
Comforting the sinner in me-
Painfully peaceful,
as I inch closer to his Domain.

Five Lashings,
The body grows heavy with regret.
Angels weeping in the archway clearing,
Begging for the whippings to cease.
A Silent God, waiting in the confession booth, omnipresent, unyield-
ing,
Demanding blood from my bones.

Six Lashings…
Drowning in this never-ending Abyss…
The leather is numb,
Is it over,
Or has it just begun?

…
76

With the Seventh Lash lying in wait…

...

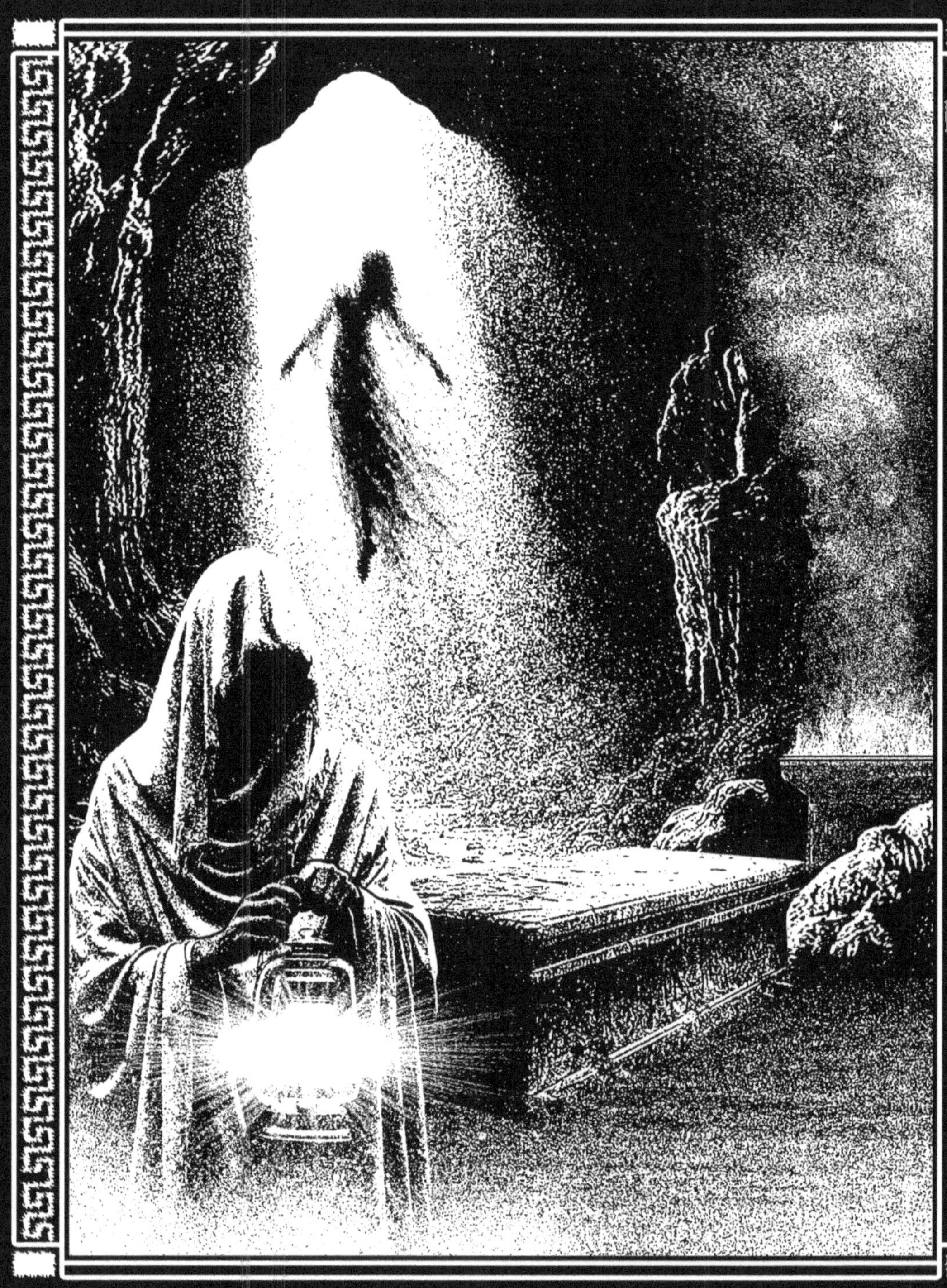

Spelunking

Delving into this ghastly decrepit crypt of dead memories and long-
lost lovers,
Your vices hold true in the torch light.
The comfort of others to blind the visage of lost,
An empty heart takes root.

Who has entered my eternal grave site?
What do you hope to find down here in my tomb?

Lives lost,
Corpses rot,
Fractured Memories float in the nothingness abyss.
Moans of the damned in the distance….

Cold, murky, dank.

Dead memories bubble to your surface.
Searching through stone caskets only to find the decay left behind.
You didn't honestly expect to find life down here, did you?

The shadows flow smoothly around your shaded skin.
Deep earthy eyes,
Such beauty beholden within.
The explorer now turned prey….

An otherworldly monster stalks the life that has entered its domain.

Torch light wavering…
Hope fading,
Fear rising,
Running as fast as fright…
Yes…
The stench of rotting me is in the air…

My dark obsession stalks this crypt tonight....

Withered Greyed eyes glance at you from shaded corners,
Your heart's crypt,
My loving eternal home.

Such a beautiful creature-
Dark skin
Browned eyes, full of life
-
Your feminine beauty tempts even MY decaying bones...

If my heart hadn't died,
I'd say it was filled with life.

I must feast upon your love....
Little tempting mouse.

A rock thrown against your fading memories,
Distraction sets root.
Now unaware of your escape closing,
The light.. dying.

Only we remain...

My dead heart needs to feel your warmth,
My withered carcass - cold and foul,
Will life be returned?

Just one taste....
I have to know...

The ecstasy of you on my receding jaw line.
The fear in your eyes....
I bite into your succulent, sweet, fresh flesh.

Sucking into your inviting neck...

I can't control my face,
Every taste….
Every one of your breaths….

More and more ravenous my lust for you…

Your fearful gaze met with compassion and desire in mine…

Have no fear, my dear,
I'll love you in death, too…

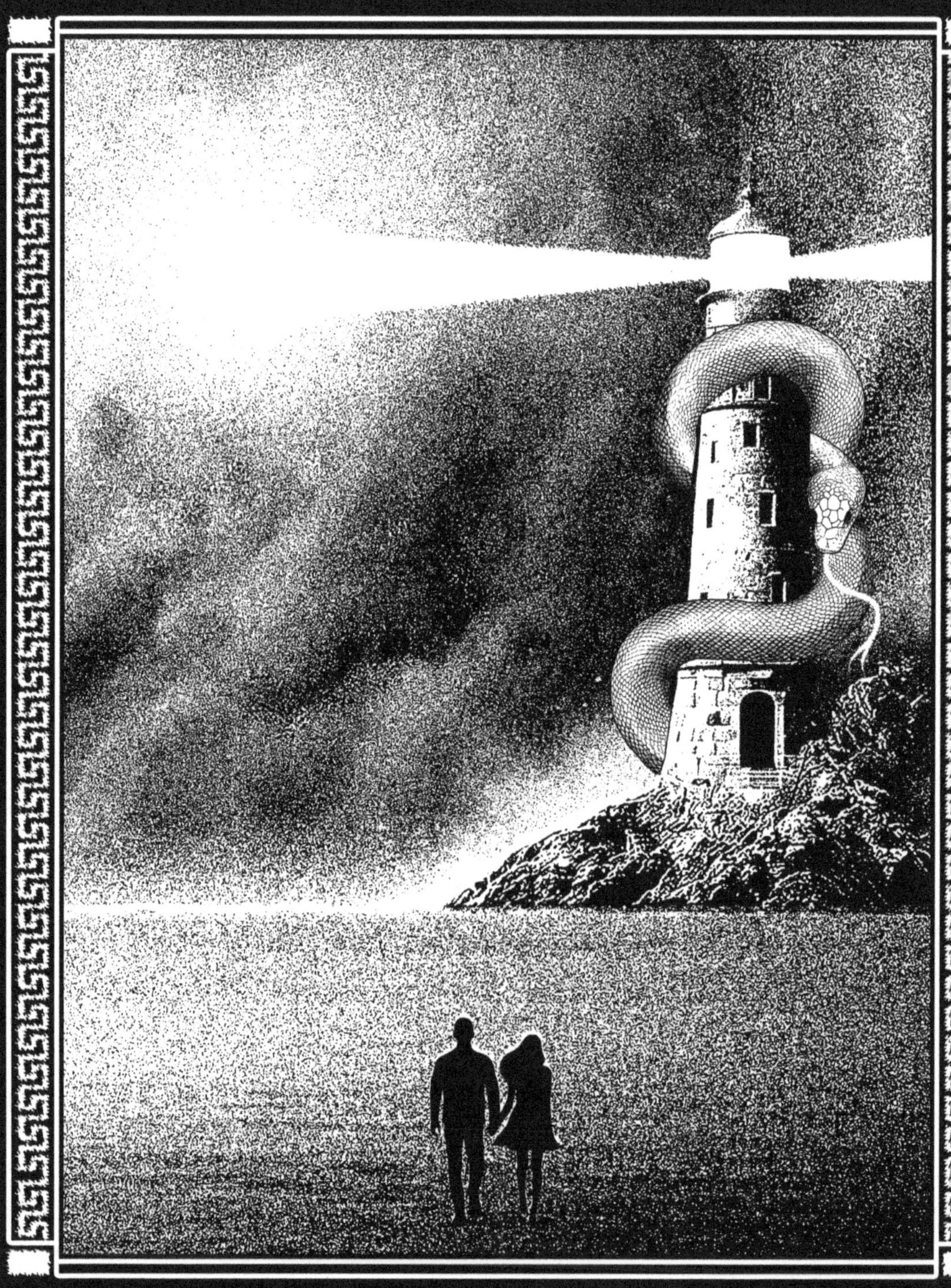

Perseverance

Through the turbulent years of our youth,
You've stood by my side steadfast to ease the tumultuous tides
crashing into our lives.
There's no way I would have survived this life without you.

The unknown hardships set before you,
You sailed headfirst into the storms.
Bearing the hurricanes,
Calming the titanic monstrosities from the depths that wished to ruin
our vessel.

The guiding star in the darkest night,
You bring safe harbor to my lost and dreary mind.
The small Schipperkes and Corgis running along the deck to check
for stowaways.

You persevered through so many perils and have come out changed.
No longer are we who we were when we first set sail.
Forever changed by the tides of time-
Persevered for the chance of our lives with each other.

The light house in my youthful monsoon,
I never would have docked home if not for your bright guiding light.

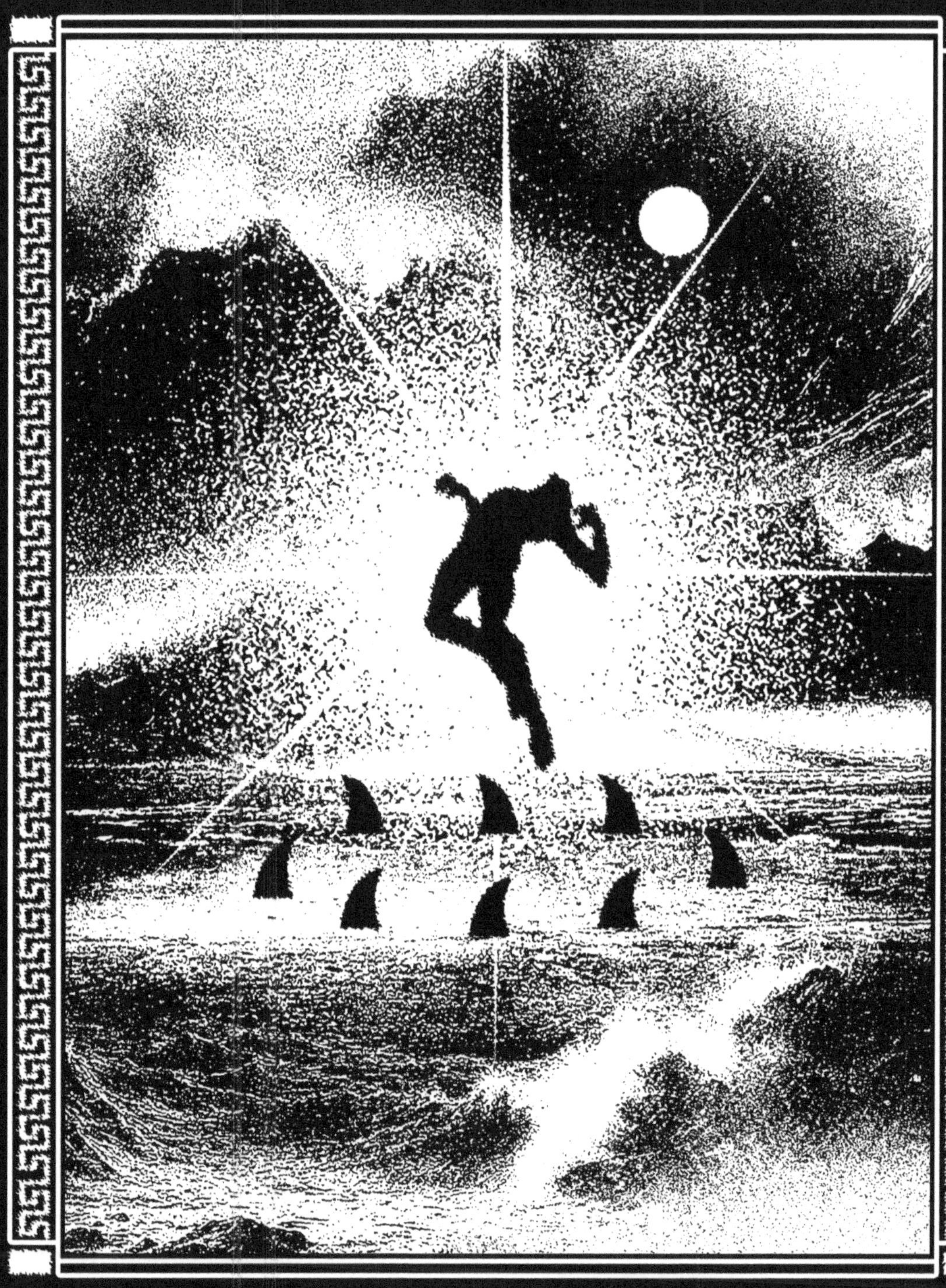

Resurrected

I've been floating along the surface of life for so long,
My bloated and decayed corpse was soulless chum for the sharks circling
the tides.

Fished out of the waters by your resilient vessel, you almost ran aground.
Unsure of the water monster you caught below the waves,
I coughed up the love I drowned upon in my dying days.

The sound of my disembodied moans as I explain the apocalypse I en-
dured,
How could you love such a monster such as I?

Ravaged by the choices of my youth,
It's evident my zombification was my own doing.

I've know the numbing cold for so long.
it's spreads through me as the poison once did before you.
Hot as ice.
Searing my flesh as it freezes solid.

Resistant to the light and life you freely sail me too,
I self-Sabotage and jump overboard into the waters of my doom.
Undeserving of the life you promise me.

Why do you follow me?
What do you see in my lifeless gaze?

Flailing wildly, you fish me back to "The Resilience" and kiss life back
into me.

The tingling fire at my lips bursts into an inferno blazing across my frigid
corpse,
Fleshing out my bones.
Evaporating my bloated and waterlogged carcass.

Ba-Dum
Crashing against my weakened chest,
My heart begins to drum.

Awakened - color returns to my grayed vision.
Warmed - the heat of your skin is evident on me.
Feeling - are these… butterflies?
Alive - the sea air fills my lungs once more.

Your kiss has Resurrected my dead heart.

Chapter 4: Revelation

In the mirror we face Ourselves,
Us,
Who we really Are.
Revel…
In the ugly truth of it all.

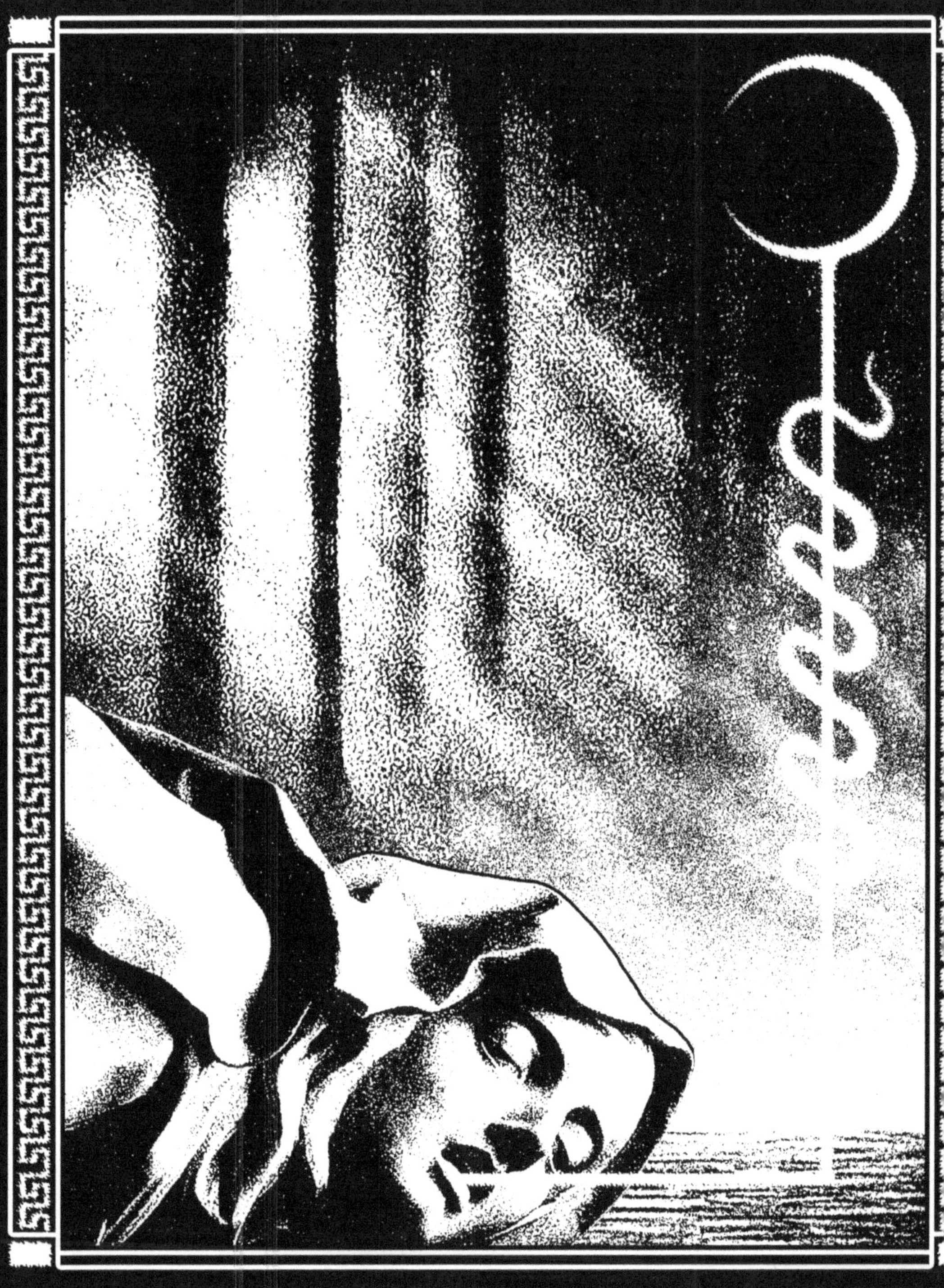

Revelation

Trekking through the Forest of my Psyche,
Laying in the earth among the fungi and creepy crawlers,
I've found sacred relics that were once lost.
My ego death is inevitable.

BOOM

Memories of your Atom Bomb flicker and explode.

The catastrophes that you inflicted on this land are the most destructive force to have ever kissed me.

The fallout slowly poisoning my sanctuary to the point of irreparable damage, I was forced to find shelter deep within the recess of my heart of stone.

Only recently have I been able to escape my paradisal prison and emerge to the above world as the shambling corpse you always envisioned me.

The fields of our life, once lush and green, lay wasting, decomposing, and rotting. The rats grow fat on the delicacies of the could-have-beens.

Echoes of your catastrophe reverberate across my mind, ringing Tinnitus, an everlasting gift.

Searching through the darkness, conversing with the shadows of my past.
They only listen.
Never responding to my words of realization and compensation.
The silence is my eternal hunger.
My nonjudicial punishment.

Epiphany- no matter how much I improve or apologize or sympthize, emphasis, naturalize, alchemize…

Nothing will reach the ears they are intended for.

An eternal struggle, to merely survive the struggle.
Entropy is eternal.
Comfort in the pain.
Maybe this is what my soul yearned for.

Just like The Poison from the land before your time, and The Cure that set me free,
You never poisoned me.

I poisoned myself.

*Authors Note: "The Poison" and "The Cure" were the first poems I ever wrote at 15 years old—echoes from a beginning that shaped everything after.

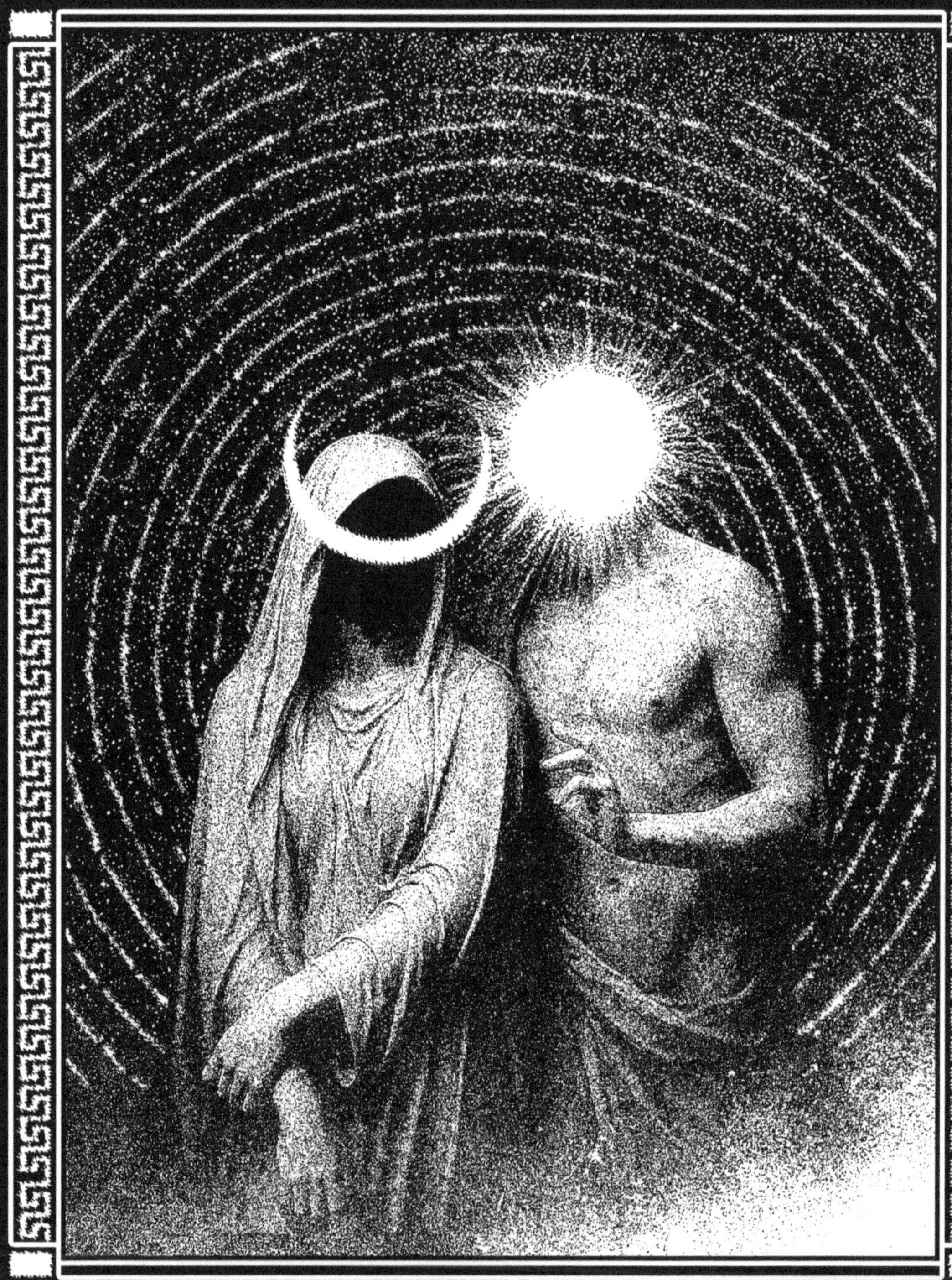

Ritual: Heilung

Preface

I speak today in hopes you will look inward.
See who you really are.
The you that is hurtful,
The you that is ugly.

We seek peace from chaos,
Escape from pain.
These are not things to hide from,
But to embrace.

Our shadow is us.
We must face ourselves to forgive ourselves.
Shadow is only the first step,
The flesh must be lived in,
We must forgive ourselves in order to
Heal ourselves.

If we close our eyes,
We'll hear the silent drums,
The whispered chants in the forest of us.

Our Ritual begins…

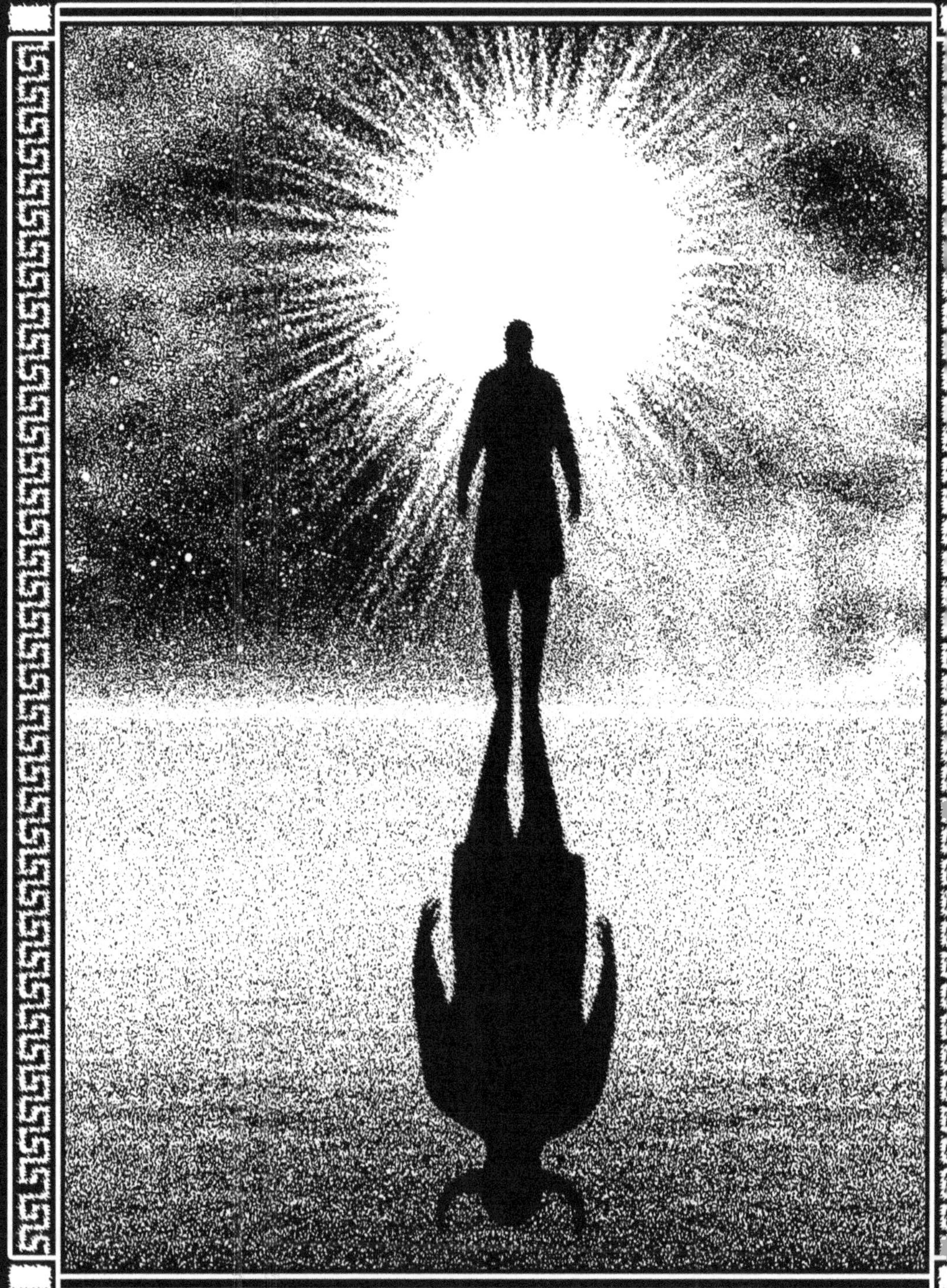

The Shadow

I call myself to this ritual circle,
I summon me.
SHADOW; who haunts me-
Bearer of my transgressions.

Wurdiz afwlītō, andōs qemanan.   1.

I see… the darkness that was me,
I see… the darkness that is me.
It follows close behind,
Eclipsing the radiant light within me.

Shadow who haunts me,
I accept the animal in me.
Shadow who stalks me,
I accept…
You are Me.

Skuggjaz inna mē, frēsan mē.   2.

In this ritual circle…
I face Me.
Fear of my own fear…
I am my own worst enemy.
The Heilung begins…

My shadow who haunts me,
Take your hideous shape…

Þurisaz wilda, andō skuggjaz.   3.

Encircled Blood Candles-
Burning,
Scattered Bones of my foul past-
Hagalas,   4.

My body-
A catalyst for my shadows form.
Flickering candle fire,
Misty Birchwood,
Moist Earth,
Rattling bones,
Swirling breeze,
The forest night is alive.

Spirits of the wild ancients,
Shaping my grief into a shaded beast;
Giant and frothing at the mouth,
Radiantly hot, yellow, feline eyes,
Hulking behemoth screeching for release.
So much anger and hate held within me.

The candle heat fades,
Illumination - Wavering and weak.
The wax melted,
The scent of burnt ash.

The shadow now complete,
Breaks through the ritual circle.
Entering me,
Showing me,
It never left me.

Sensation flows through me:
Freezing heat,
A knife's caress inside.
Eyes roll back.
I become me.

Visions…
Hurt…
Crying…
Pain suffered…

Betrayed…
Because of me.

Rivers gush down to earth from my face-

I accept the past me,
I no longer hide from the evil in me.
I forgive me for the pain I inflicted,
The younger me.

Lāþōs skīnan, þwahan unsarā.   5.

Now;
My shadow inhabits
The Wiser Me.

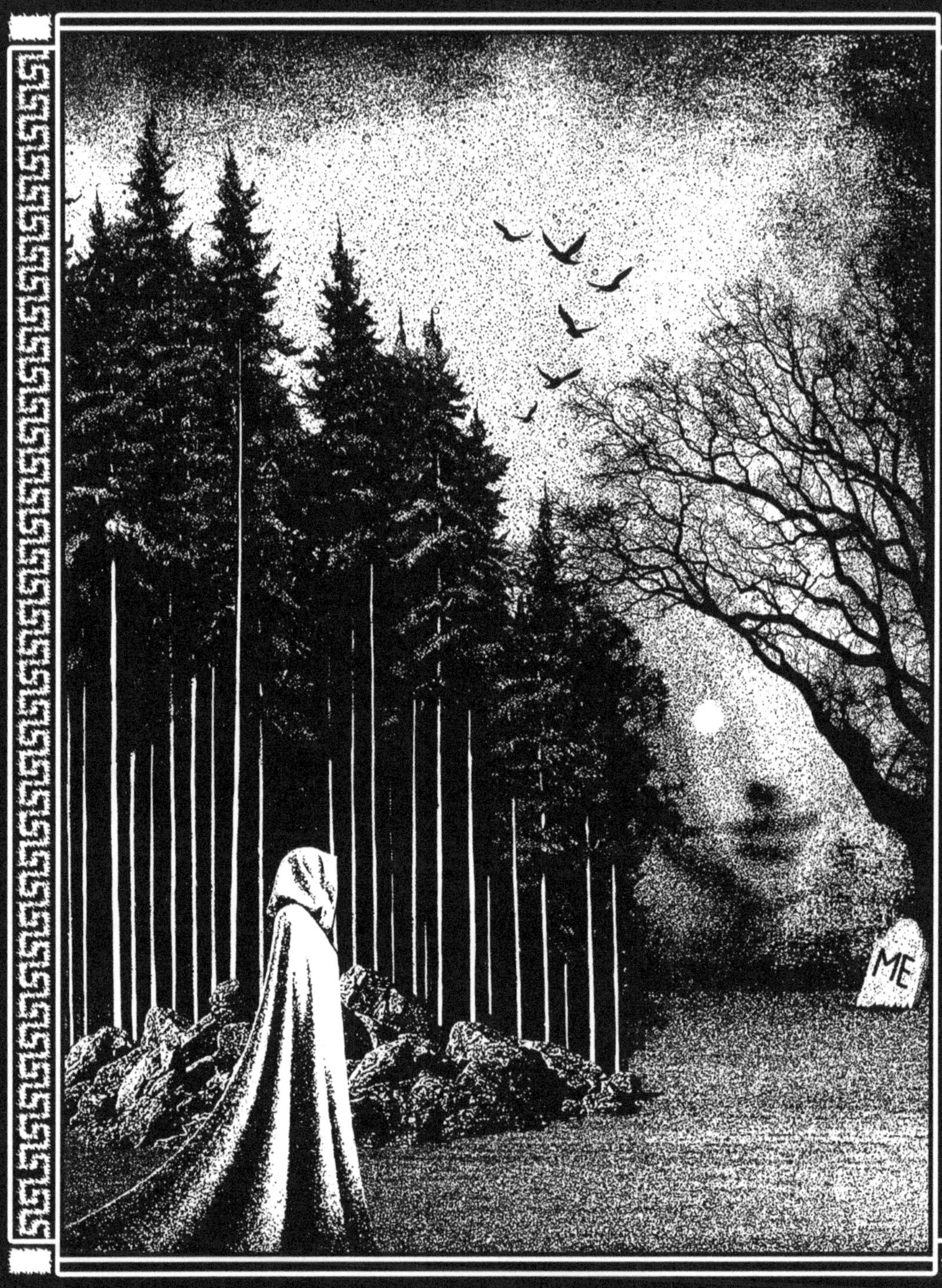

ME

The Me

Spiritual Aura glowing,
Darkness turns to gray.
The forest is still,
Goosebumps rise to the surface.

Alive and breathing.
I am flawed,
I have hurt.

I am present,
I am improving.

I have searched for God,
I am spiritual.

I have found….
Something.

It is within me.

I am human,
Not escaping my flesh prison,
But here…
On Earth,
Present in this blink of time.

Deep forest drums thrum the beat,
Beating to my heart beat.
Ritualistic sacrifice of me,
For the God within me.

Ik ben mann, līþjō, betri.   6.

My flesh must confront the afflicted,
My flesh must ask for forgiveness.

My flesh must accept the outcome,
Dictated by a past lifetime.

With this body- I have hurt.
With this body- I will heal.
Our hands are the creators of our
Destiny.
Our feet are the instruments to Our destination.

Take the first steps
To Heilung.

Handuns frabūtan, fōtuns wrastjan.   7.

I.
Am.
Heilung.

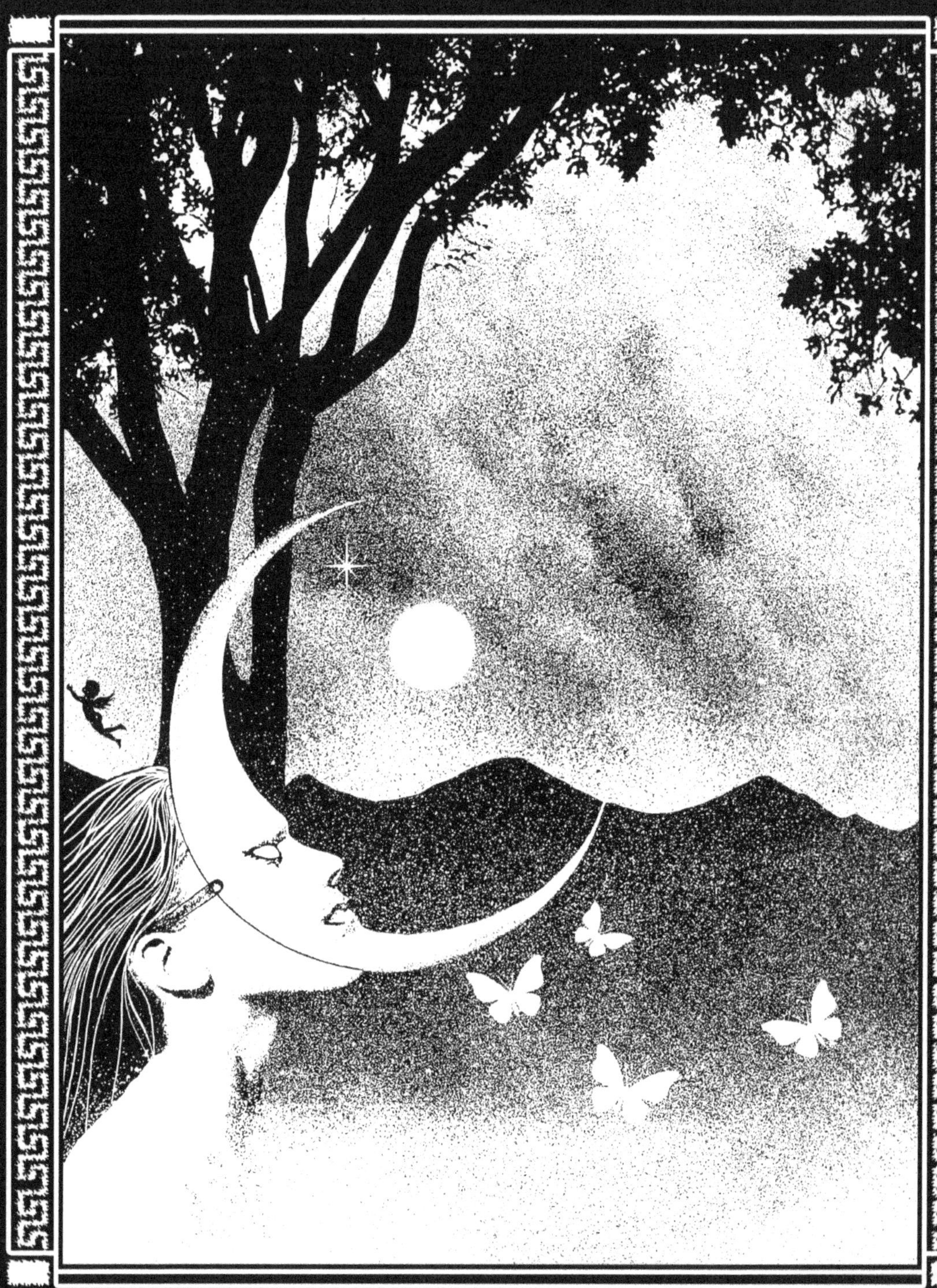

Heilung

We cannot improve until we heal,
This I know to be true.
We must face ourselves,
The shadow, the flesh.

Skuggjaz jah līuhata meldijan.   8.

Heilung cannot begin within us without us,
We must accept ourselves and continue to improve.

Þwahan unsarā, heilaz bringan.   9.

Our rituals—
For love,
For children,
For peace,
For yourself…
We must complete.

Wurdiz rīnan, andōs faurhwītan.   10.

Healing is a return,
A return of the shadow,
Of the flesh,
Of the self.

Hugiz, līkoz, sawol… sindā.   11.

We must forgive…

We are all…
Heilung.   12.

Proto-Germanic Translations for "Ritual: Heilung"

1. The threads of fate unwind, spirits arise.
2. Shadow within me, devour me.
3. The wild beast, the spirit of shadow.
4. Rune associated with Destruction and Transformation
5. Let light shine, cleanse us.
6. I am human, flawed, improving.
7. Hands create, feet journey.
8. Shadow and light must merge.
9. Cleanse us, bring healing.
10. Fate flows, spirits guide forward.
11. Mind, body, soul… are one.
12. Healing

Chapter 5: Ascension

Rising from the shadows,
We now understand…
We were never lost,
We just couldn't see us for us.
Breathe and release.
You are healing…
You are free…

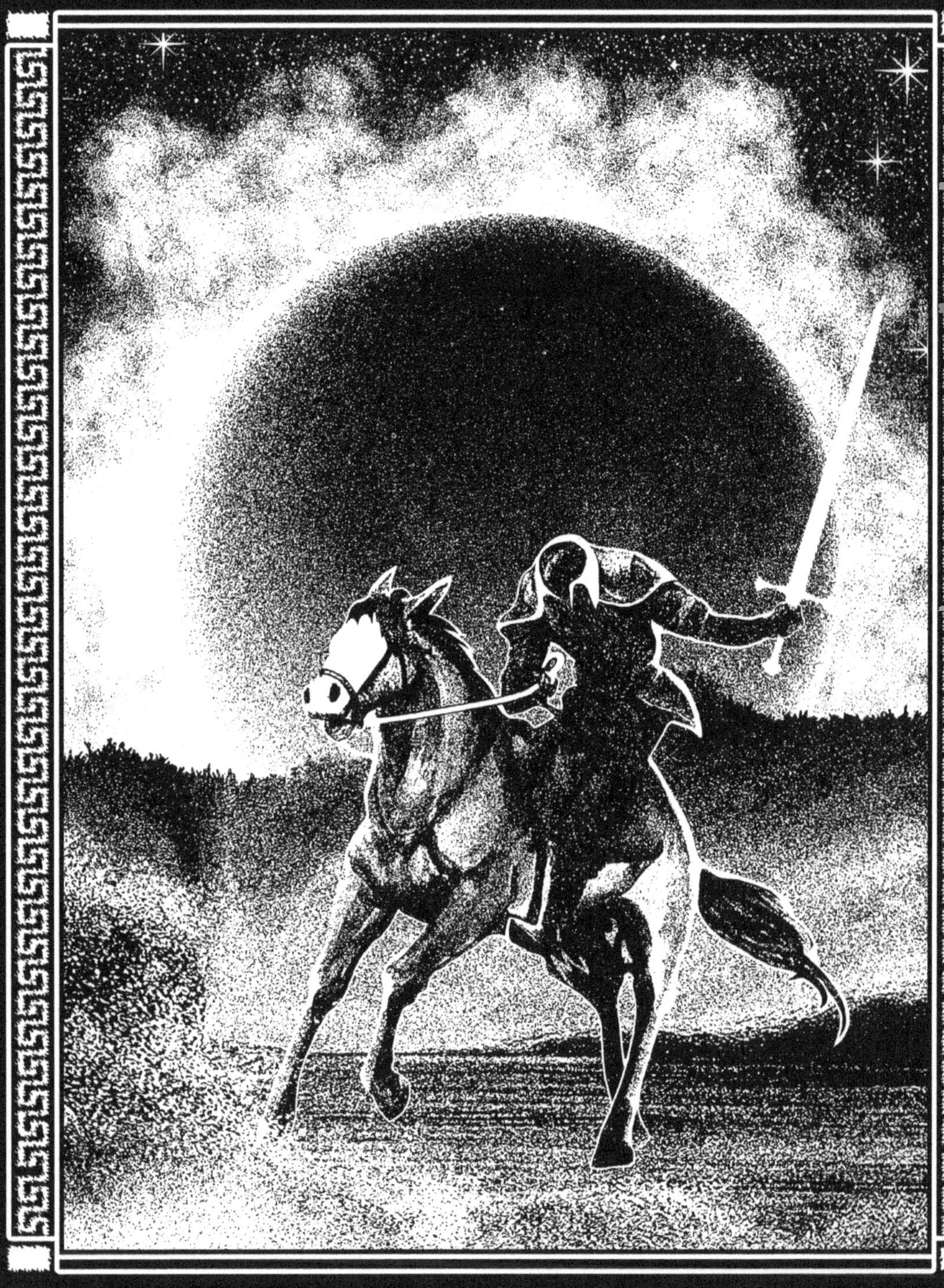

The Horseman

Chill blankets the earth once more,
The season of dread returned.
Freezing flame rising in the night,
Born by that Headless Horseman.

Cold and radiantly Blue,
Ghostly white,
Blindingly bright.
Can you see it?
Yes- you're right- it is the moon.

In The Darkness we find our dreams,
In the bask of the freezing moonlight,
we are tested steadfast against the coming end, brought swiftly by
that hulking mass.
Unstoppable-
Immovable-
The Headless Horseman Rides.

Riding on his steed of decay-
Giant, hulking, diseased, and foul.
A beast to match the White Riders Aura.
A beautiful Deceiver-
Swaying you from your Dreams.
"What will you sacrifice for your desires?"

Stand against the blinding light of the darkness,
Face The Hand of God.
Betray the set path before you.
Prove your Fate is Yours alone to determine.

Bask in the freezing moonlight.
Steal yourself against the blazing cold.
Entropy staged as the battlefield-

Fight, Berserk! against the closing Dark.

Prove your Dreams are worthy of being Dreamt.

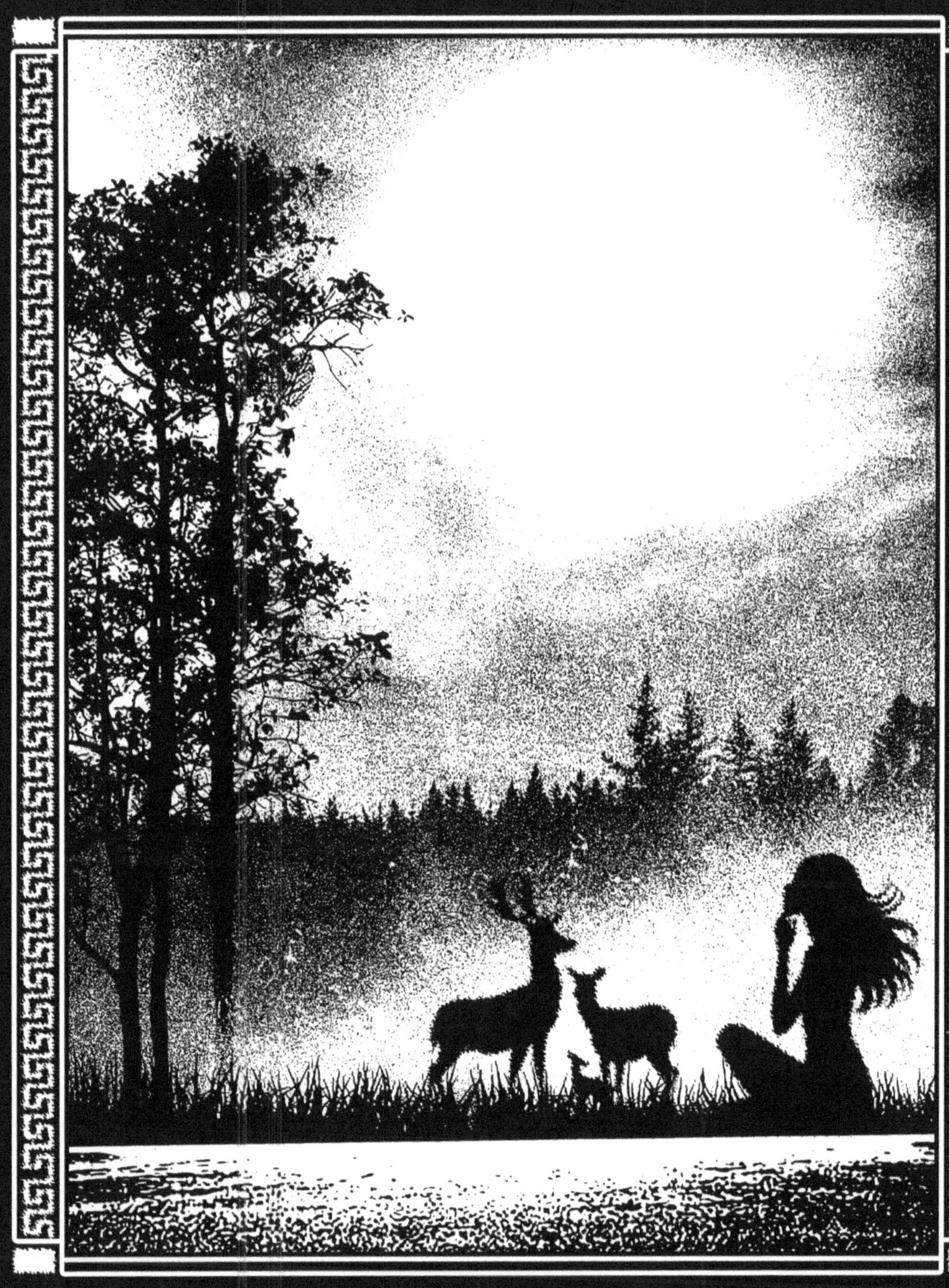

Hope

The sun shines radiantly bright on the green grass meadows that now
populate my once desolated wasteland of a mind;
Your beautiful visage frolicking through the shrubbery and loving
the wildlife.

The way you pick the overgrown weeds from the withered flow-
ers and replant my untended soil touches parts of my soul that was
thought to be entombed and buried underneath all the destruction
that can be seen past the pasture.

Seeing you so lovingly enjoying your time in my mind and free to
express yourself reminds me of a younger me.
Someone who was pure and who had witnessed a pain like this be-
fore.

I can see the tears that you have shed before coming here.
I can see the pain you also learned to love.
Our scars bleed through each other's delicate touch.

You are the culmination of events of a Winters past who never es-
caped their storm.
A memory seared deeply into my soul.

You bring hope and life to my wasteland of a mind.
The rivers flow blue and the meadow animals return to once again
populate the land.

You are loved here.
I hope you'll make your home here.

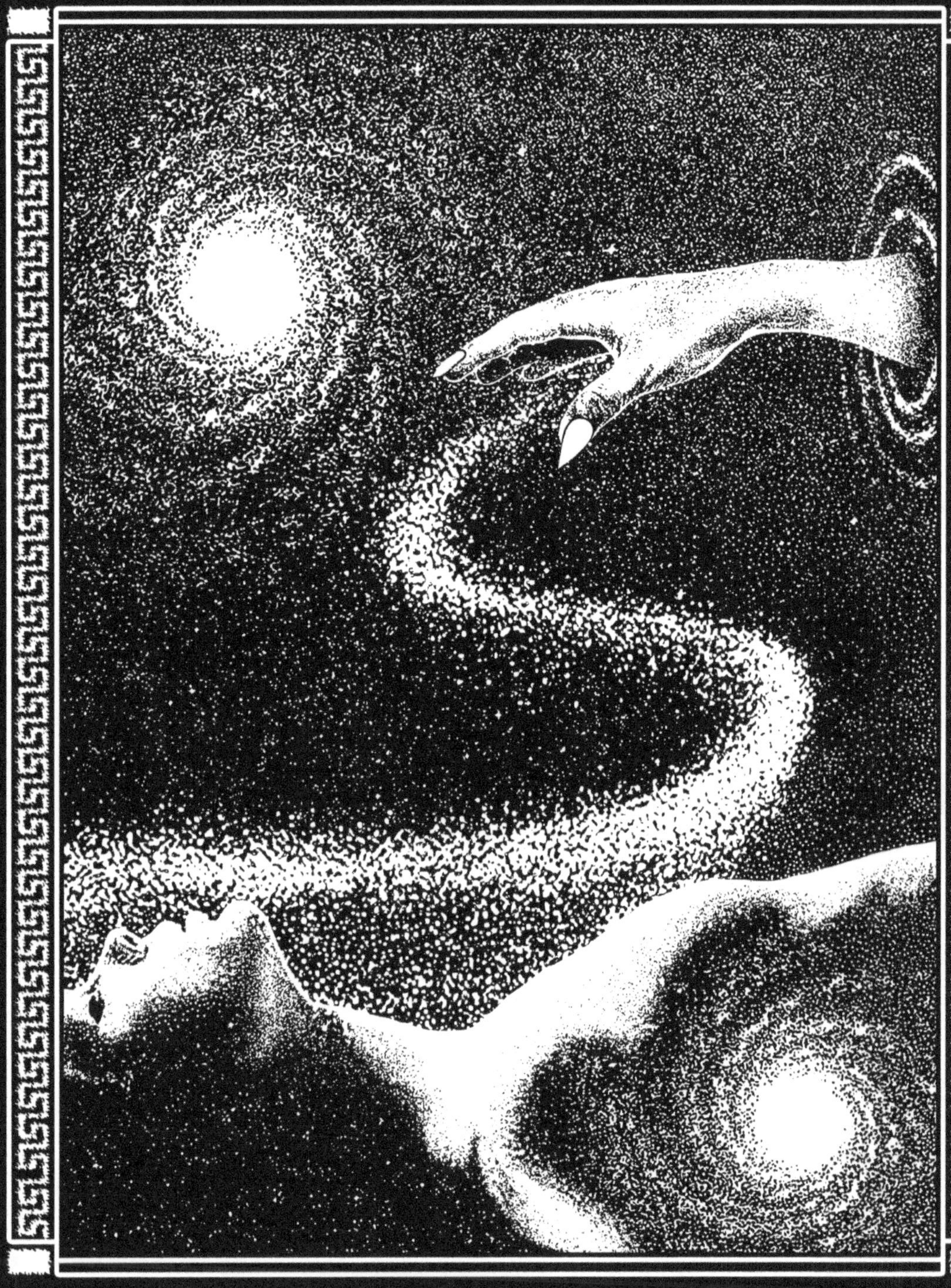

Illusion

Embodying the visage of my nurture,
My body developed by nature.
I know in the eternal everything,
This is an Illusion.

The Spirit, The Soul,
experiencing the Universe itself -
all at once, none at all.

I'm alive and breathing.

I know this is an Illusion.
My body knows it-
My Spirit feels it.

My pain is a mist covered veil-
Woven tightly,
Elegantly-
Shrouding over me.

In you, I find me and me and me and me-
Again, and again there I am,
Again, and again there you are.
In me, you find you and you and you and you.

In all of Us-
Mirrors,
Reflecting Eternity.

Closing my eyes,
Breathing deep.

Exhale your Shadow-
Embrace your Anima/Animus,
It's finally opening.

With my eyes wide shut,
Now I truly see.

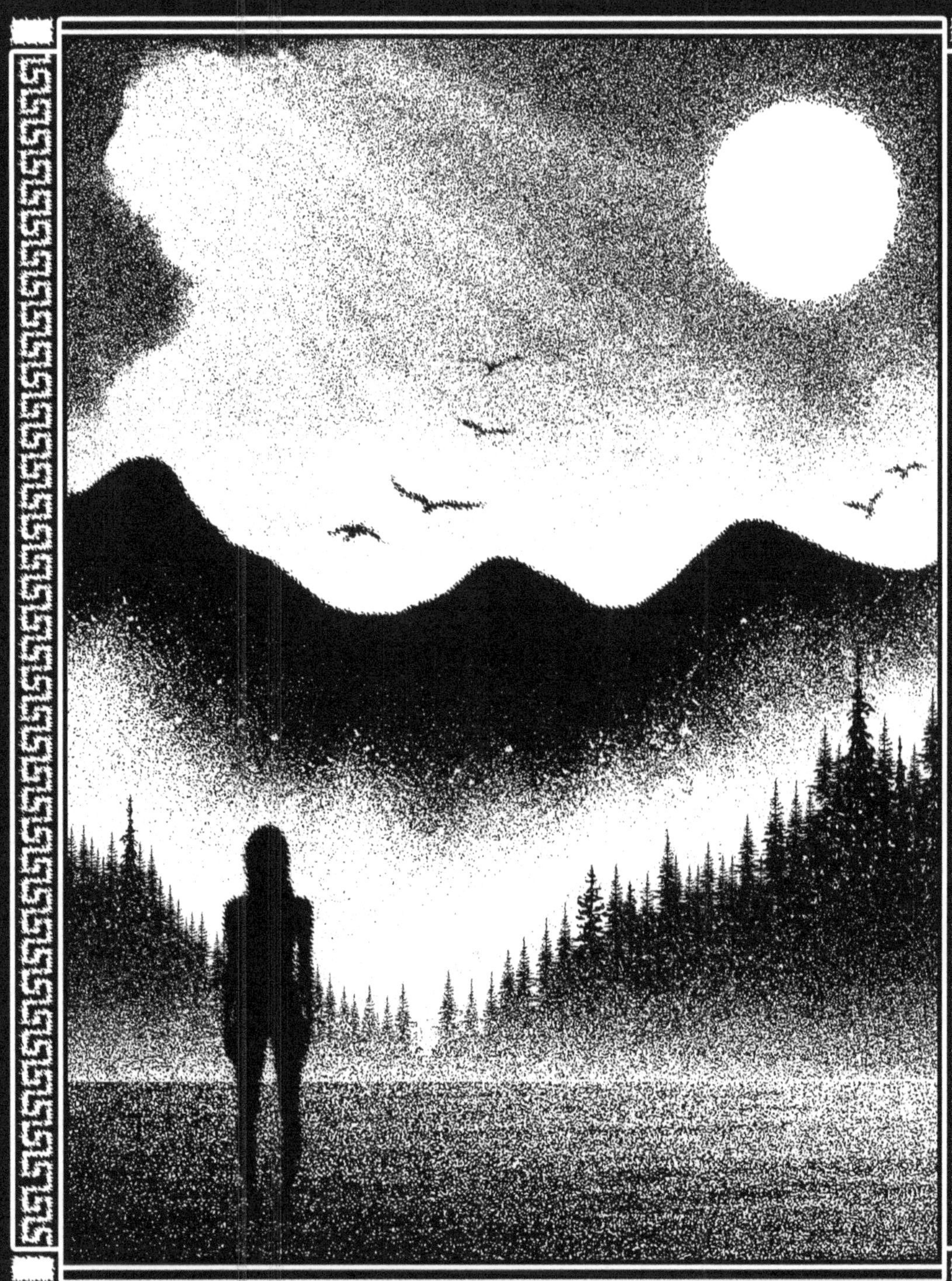

Grounded

It's good to Feel,
It's good to Need,
It's good to Breathe.

But once your fantasies are over,
it's Time to return to Ground-
Down in Reality.

It's good to Feel the Earth beneath your feet,
Where the soil is Fertile and Cool-
Mother Earth Nurtures eagerly.

It's good to Need to just Be,
The desire to Exist means your Heart is Beating.

It's good to Breathe,
The Air exhales Forgiveness of all our Sins.

It's good to Feel,
To Need,
To Breathe.

Only in Reality can we
become One in
The Universe's Native Tongue.

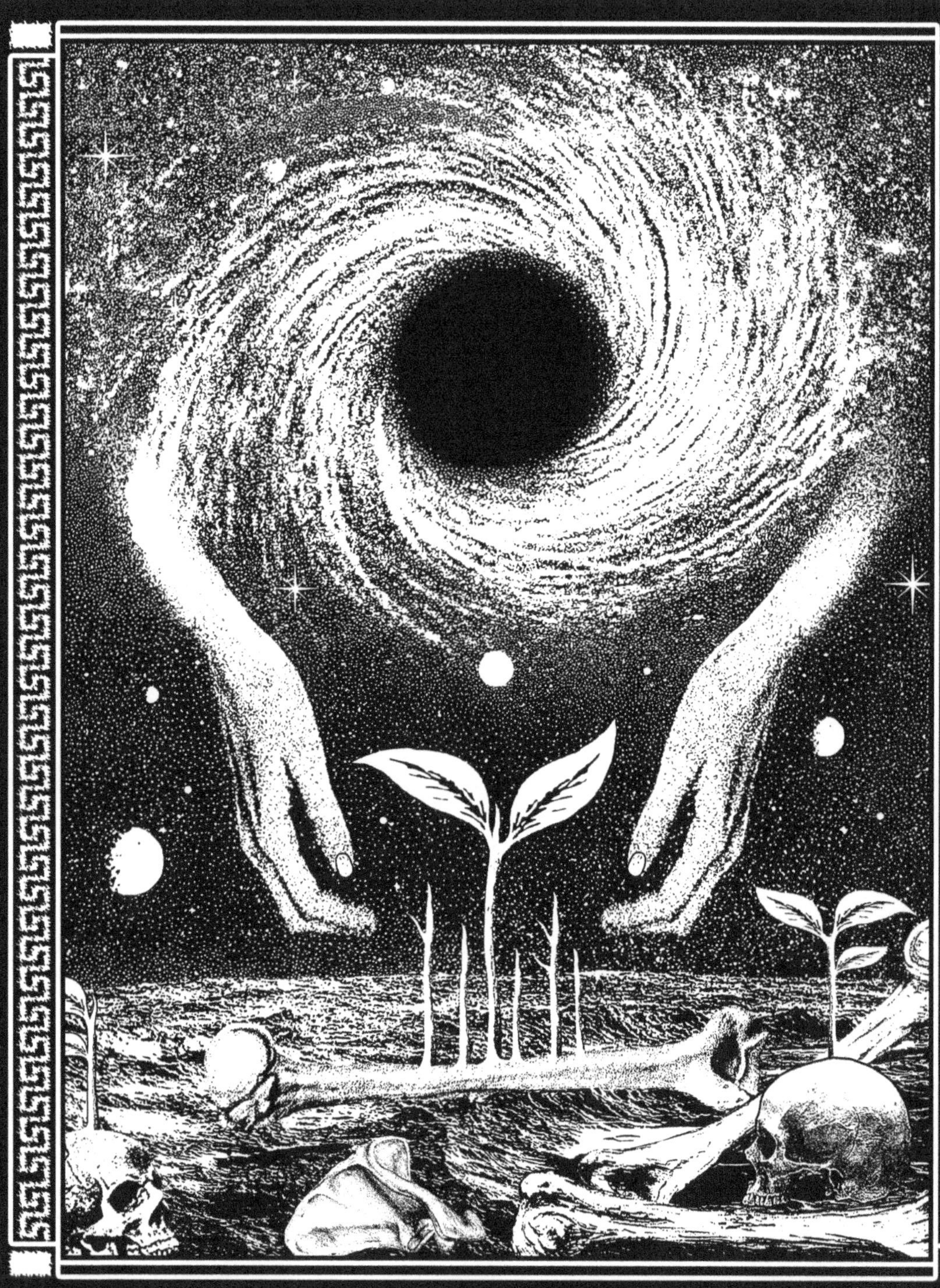

Bones

In the infinite nothingness of time and space,
A drop of life sprouted and placed.
The universe unfurled to exist,
Here on earth, you luckily lived.

Tick… Tock…

Dust to dust,
Our flesh consumed by the marching of time,
Nothing more than food for the earth.

My atoms combined,
For us to experience life at the same time.

Midnight Hour strikes noon;
Ringing explosively through the moons.

Before existence we are just star dust,
Intermingling in one another's gravity.

The building blocks for bones,
Yes- my essence knows you still.

Astral spirits bound to the flesh,
Star soul,
I remember you.

Eternity before,
My bones met you.

Eternity after.
My bones will remember you…
Remember you in the quiet darkness of space.

The Midnight Mass has ended.

The shadows… Witnessed,

The Bones… Burned,

Rebuilt from the soul up.

Go forth now,

As the wiser you,

The better you…

Heal.

Extra Content

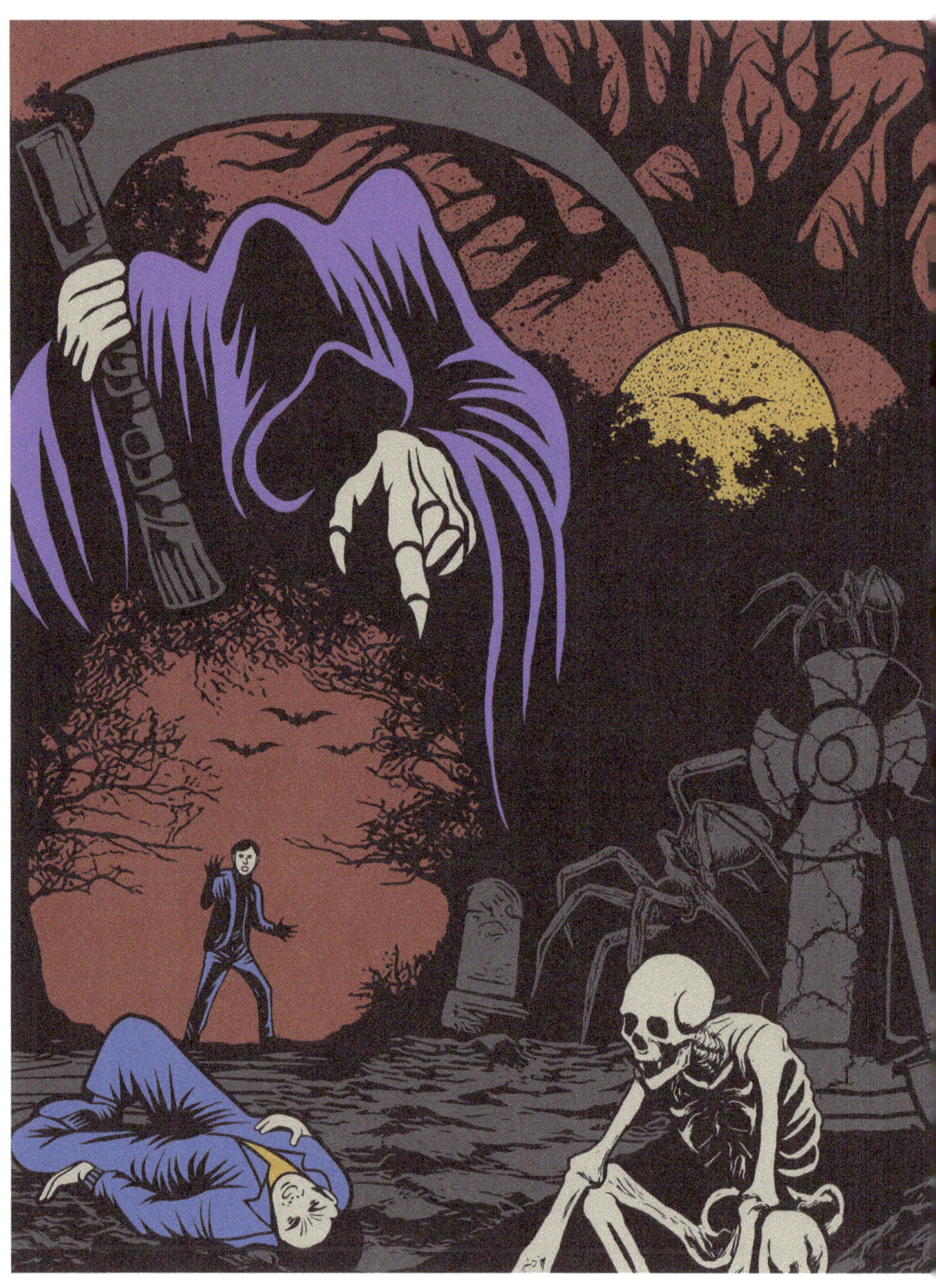

Skinwalker early design (art by Sarah Fazriah Instagram @voidofdoom__)

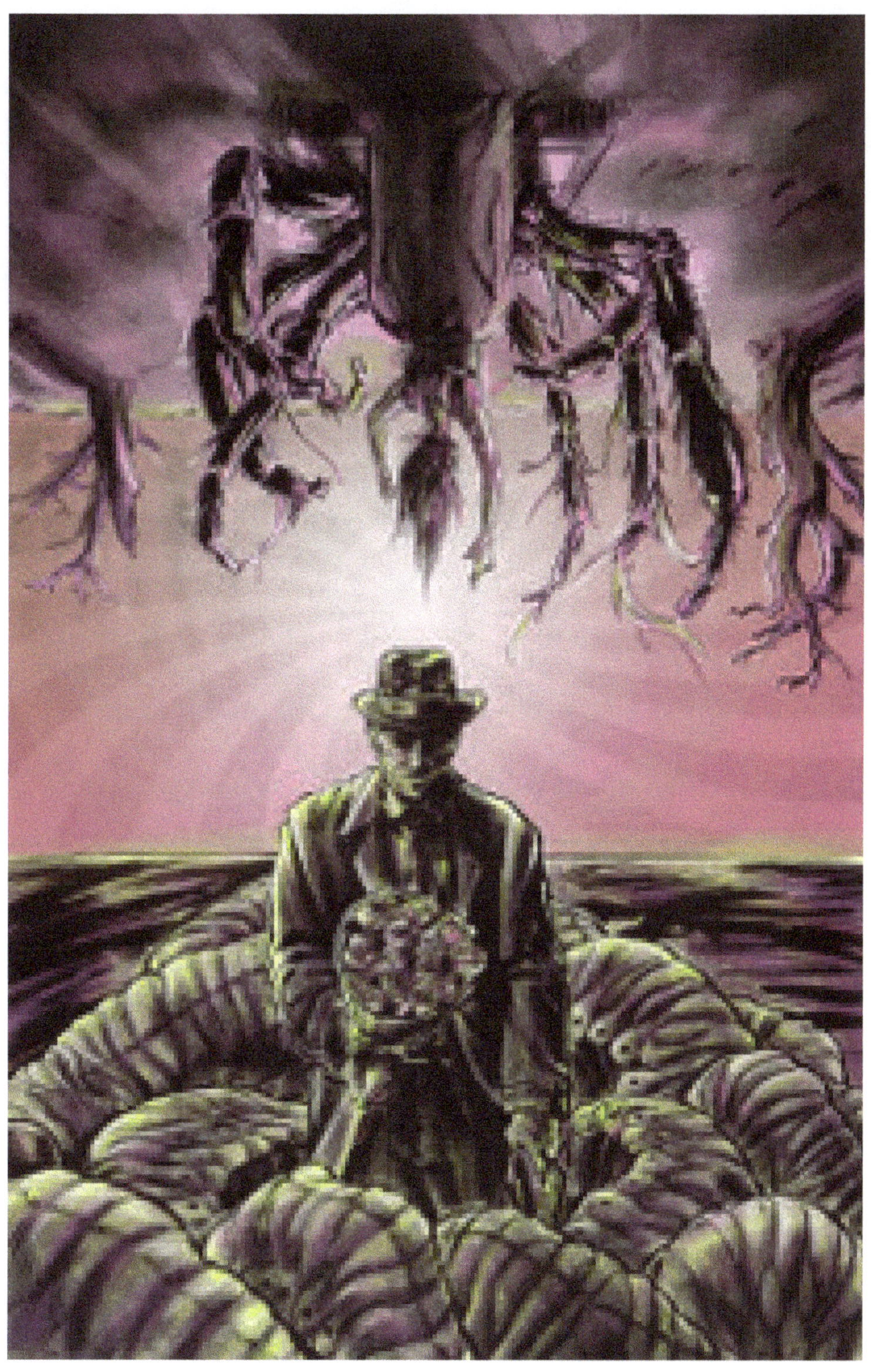

Skin Walker Alternate Design (by J Matthias Lissak Instagram @jmlissa)

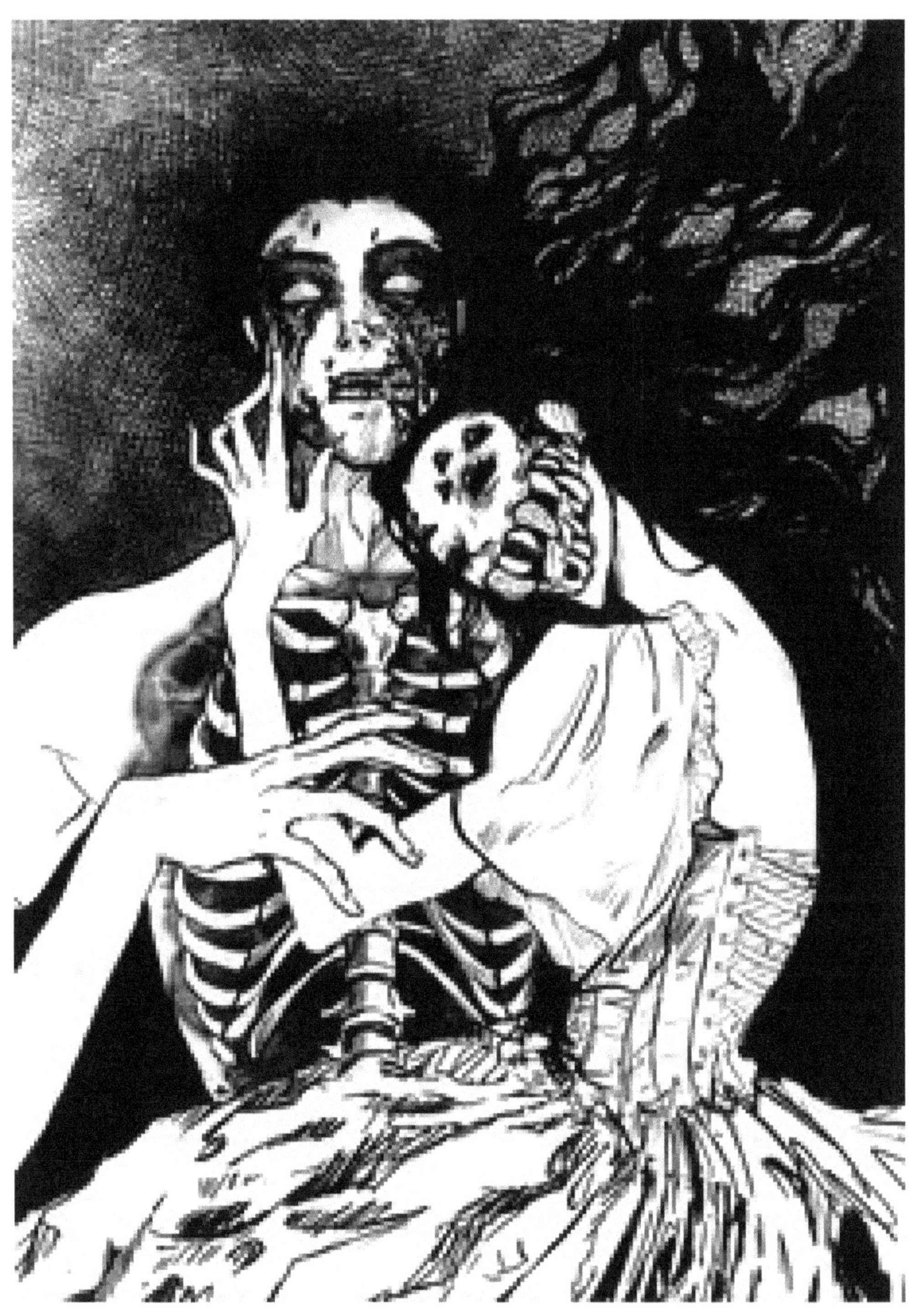

Skin Walker Alternate Design (By Camille Gomez Instagram @art.screaming-forfairies)

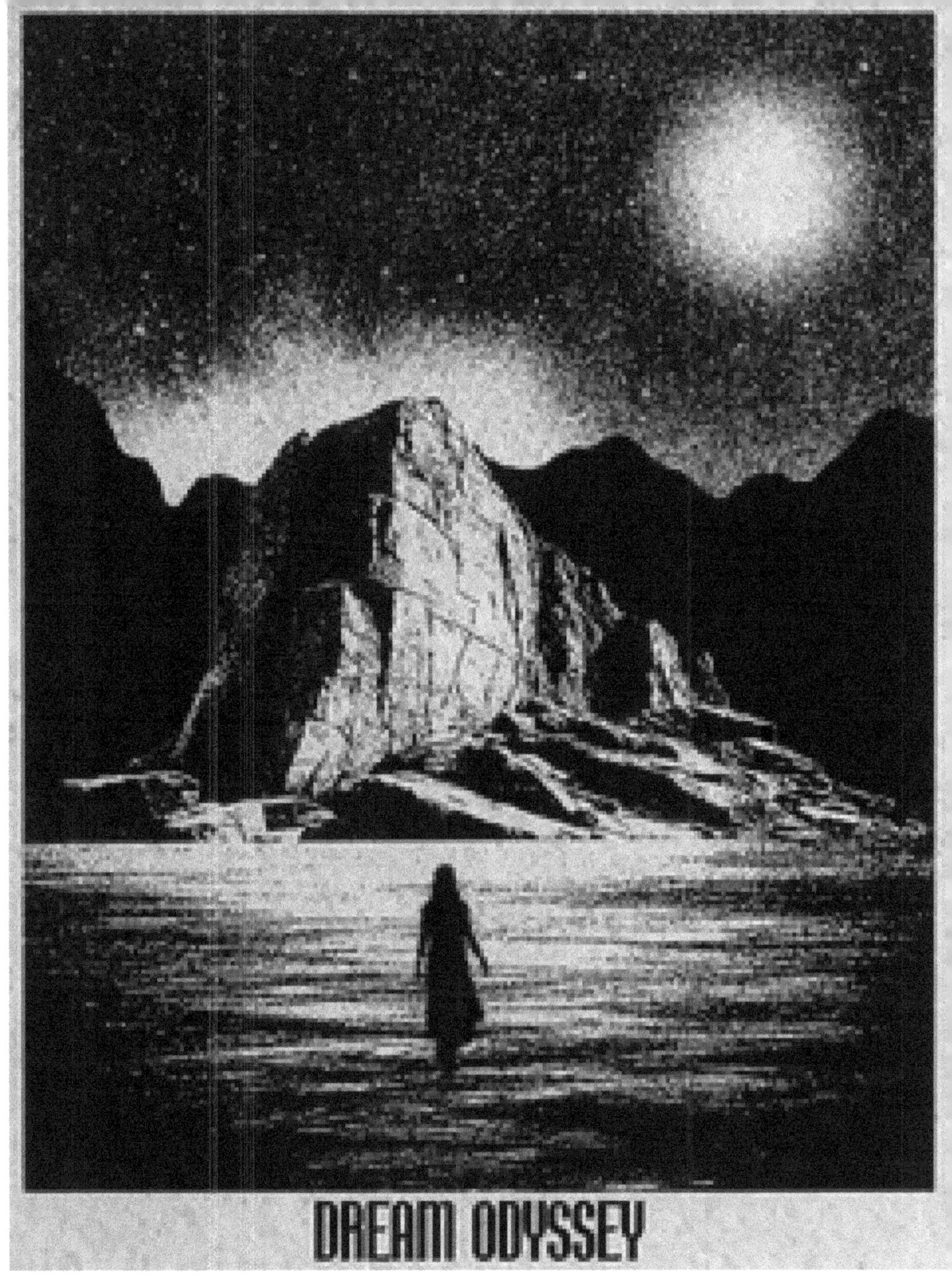

Dream Odyssey (Art by Sarah Fazriah Instagram @mvddrak_atmospheric)
(Sarah commissioned me to make a poem for an art piece she worked on outside of the book)

Dream (Dream Odyssey part 1)

The terrors of day put the fright into me,
So eagerly I wait to lay my head to sleep,
The bed of solitude is mine to take,
My comfort in my home,
My only escape.

Entering the softness of my sheets,
A ceiling fan.
My window cracked,
A cold breeze cools my mind.

The expected weighted terror upon my chest
Tick… Tock… Tick… Tock….
The midnight shadow man is near.

I hope I dream this night,
Save me from my blight.
A memory played within my mind,
Echoes of daylight memories,
Still bright.

Shutting my brown eyes,
The darkness takes me deep,
Down into the depths of my dreams.

Encroaching darkness encircles me,
Stutters and steps,
Ghostly jerks and sweats,
Falling in my sleep,
A restless mess.

Finally,

Peace at last,
My mind is at ease,
And now my Dream Odyssey can begin.

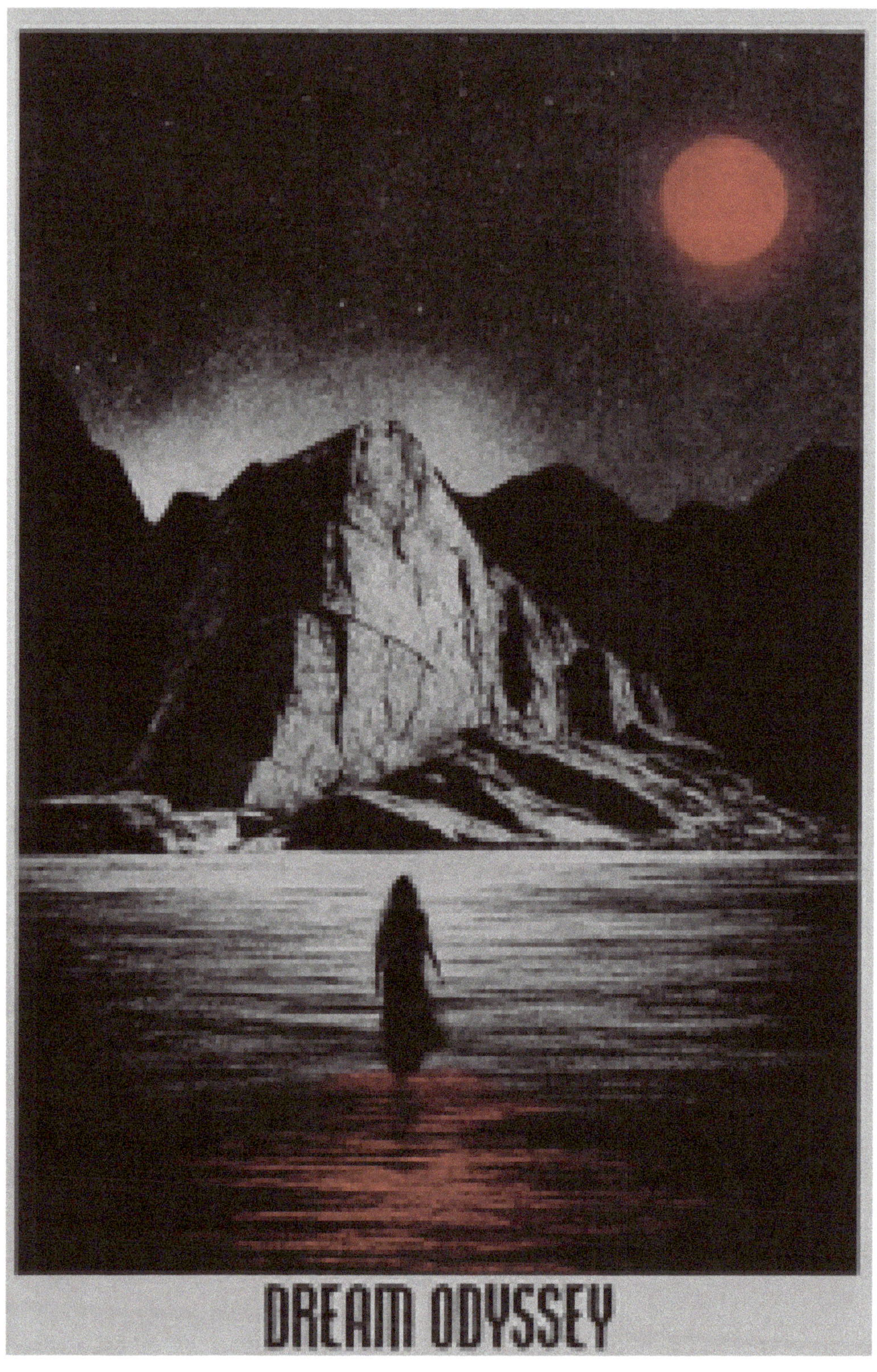

DREAM ODYSSEY

Odyssey (Dream Odyssey part 2)

Falling…. Falling…. Falling...
Splashing into the river of my dreams.
Soaked wet with dread,
A river styx of memories.

The terror of my day will not be swayed,
Followed me still,
Deep into my dreams,
My only escape will be my Odyssey.

The moon - silver and bright,
Hanging mournfully in the sky.
Pouring its soul down into my eyes.

Wading through the lost souls of sleep,
Sticking to my feet,
There lays dry land,
A meadow.

The shadow man waiting nearby-
Of course he is here.

My chest is heavy,
My feet are slow.
As expected,
My weighted fear draws near.

The muck of me,
Sloshing and slopping through the gunk and bile,
I follow my path through my meadow.
Devoid of life - a self reflection.

Pitter… Patter… Pitter… Patter…
Terror draws close,

Shadow man,
Crawling down below.
A mountain of salvation,
High into the sky,
I can reach the weeping moon,
End its cry.

My tumultuous climb,
The summit is there,
Just a bit more,
Before my horror is no more.

Clip… clop…
The Shadow Man breaks.
Always one step ahead,
Waiting for me and my death.
He's not fear,
He's fate…

Standing atop this mountain peak,
Luna, she weeps for me.
Facing the darkness of my mind.
The Midnight Shadow Man and I.

His crooked mouth screeches,
My own soul reaches out.
Meeting face to face to face.

Luna now red with dread,
Falls from the sky,
And even the Stars,
Way up high.

Divinity and I,
If just to see…

The Midnight Man is Me…

The midnight hour has passed,
The morning sun breaks dawn.
The shadows of my mind burned away,
But one horror still remains.

Now past my dreams…

Eyes opened wide,
During daylight hours,
A vessel…

The Shadow Man Sleeps deep,
Deep beneath my skin.

This is not a sermon… it's a summoning.

Midnight Mass: Poetic Scripture for the Broken Soul is a journey into the cathedral of shadows within us all. Across five chapters — Genesis, Descent, Abyss, Revelation, and Ascension — these poems lead you through the darkest corridors of love, loss, pain, and transformation.

Each section is a rite of passage: the birth of hope, the fall into despair, the confrontation with our inner demons, the rituals of a revelation, and finally, the rise toward acceptance and self-understanding. The words within are not here to preach, but to guide — to hold a candle to the places we fear to enter alone.

This collection is for anyone walking their own path of healing, for those who have loved and lost, raged and endured, and emerged changed. It is a ritual in ink, a mirror to your soul, and a reminder that only by facing the darkness can we ever truly rise.

The bells are tolling. The Midnight Mass… begins.

This is NOT a religious book,
but it is spiritual.
This collection of poems
will take you through a dark
journey of Love, loss, pain,
suffering, understanding,
and acceptance.
Only after we face our mon-
sters can we truly begin to
understand who we are.

Let the Midnight Mass…
begin.

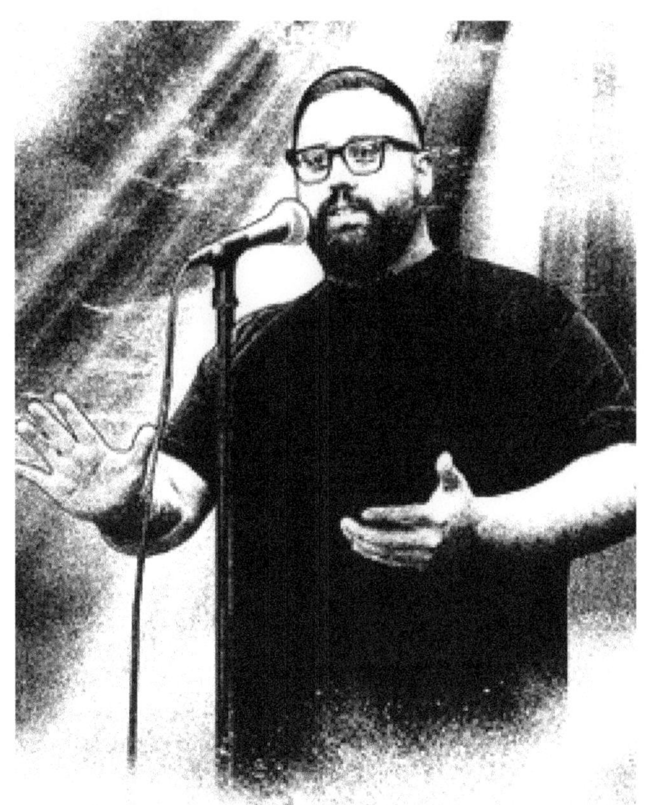

Daniel Villanueva is an Orange County, California poet inspired by Edgar
Allan Poe, Dante Alighieri, and the beauty of the macabre. His work has
been featured by the SoCal Poetry Collective and performed at intimate
poetry gatherings throughout Southern California. You can follow him on
Instagram at @HauntedQuills.

Publishers Note

Daxson Publishing was created to help marginalized artists and their allies publish their work, so the world can hear their voice. The vision for this publishing house is to help people get their work out there, and not have them struggle finding their way through the publishing process. Everyone's voice deserves to be heard, and we are here to help. If you are interested in submitting a manuscript, email daxsonpublishing@gmail.com. Support our cause by buying books from daxsonpublishing. com.

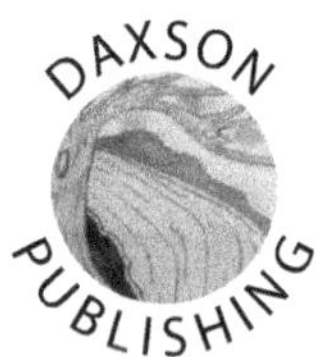